Basic Computing

Taking the Fear Out of Using a Computer

For the beginning computer user or anyone currently not getting the full potential out of their daily computer use. The Focus is on Windows 7 operating system, but all users will benefit.

By Mike Bodenhafer

ISBN: 1460978927

ISBN-13: 978-1460978924

About the Author

Mike Bodenhafer purchased his first computer, a Commodore 64, back in 1985 and has been computing ever since. Taking a different route than most kids of the time, he was more fascinated with the productivity side of the computer than the gaming side, writing small programs that did little more than a calculator. It was not long before curiosity got the best of him and he opened the case on the computer to look inside. Thus began a long period of computer repair. For years, many friends and family encouraged Mike to start a career in the computer industry, but with a young family and only a high school education, he never overcame the fear of the risk. Finally, with the kids grown and the economic recession of 2008, Mike found himself without a job, and the opportunity to go to college presented itself.

Attending Ivy Tech Community College, Mike obtained an Associate of Applied Science in Computer Information Technology at the end of 2010. During that same time he opened PMCreation, a computer and surveillance service and sales company. In a short time he saw a need for computer training, so working with a local continuing education academy he began to teach evening classes. With training materials constantly becoming outdated due to the rapid progression of the industry, Mike found it necessary to write his own book and soon added author to his list of accolades.

➢ *It has been said that with all of the time savings that have been created by using the computer, we are becoming lazy. I say that it is more a question of what we do with the time we have saved. Spend your savings wisely and your life will be better.*

o *Mike Bodenhafer*

Table of Contents

What is a Computer?

A computer is an electronic device that manipulates information or "data." It has the ability to store, retrieve, and process data. You can use a computer to type documents, send email, and surf the Internet. You can also use it to handle spreadsheets, accounting, database management, presentations, games, and more.

That is the simple definition of a computer, but the truth is, computers touch our everyday lives in many ways so it would be hard to define them in one paragraph. Whether you realize it or not, using the definition above, you most likely own and operate many computers. Computers play an important role in our lives. When you withdraw cash from an ATM, scan groceries at the store, or use a calculator, and even drive your car, you're using a type of computer. Although most of us think of computer's as the desktops or laptops we have on our desk, the truth is that "embedded" computers found in other devices are much more numerous.

Although all of this is important to know, for the purposes of this book we will limit our discussions to the more visible laptops and desktops.

The first electronic computer, the Electronic Numerical Integrator and Computer (ENIAC), was developed in 1946. It measured 18 feet by 80 feet and weighed 30 tons.

All types of computers consist of two basic parts – **hardware** and **software**.

Hardware

Hardware is any part of your computer that you can touch. The case, the monitor, the keyboard and mouse are the common and most visible, but there is much more. Inside the case you will find the meat of the computer.

Hardware of a Modern Personal Computer

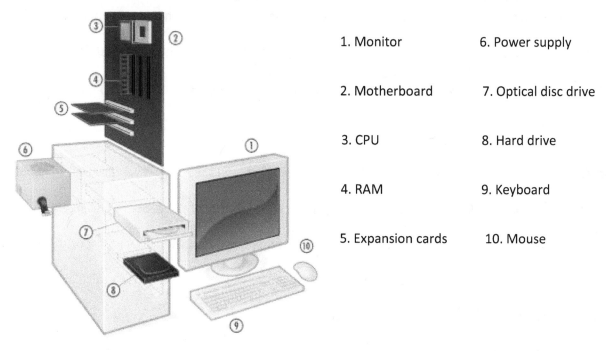

1. Monitor	6. Power supply
2. Motherboard	7. Optical disc drive
3. CPU	8. Hard drive
4. RAM	9. Keyboard
5. Expansion cards	10. Mouse

Figure 1

The best way for a beginner to think about a computer is to compare it to something commonly known. I think that we can all understand the external parts so let's look inside.

The Motherboard can be compared to our interstate highway system. As information from your input devices (keyboard and mouse) need to travel through the computer to be processed, it will move through the circuitry of the motherboard. The circuits on the motherboard range in size from the super highways down to the small state roads and even city streets, which cannot be seen by the naked eye. There are intersections, off ramps and even some dead ends. As the information moves through this system of turns and twists you might ask how it knows which turns to take. This is all controlled by the Central Processing Unit (CPU).

The CPU is similar to the brain in that it makes decisions based on a set of information or instructions that it has been told. We will get deeper into these instructions in the software section, but for now just think of the CPU as the master of all hardware.

Memory could be compared to your inbox and outbox sitting on your desk. It is a temporary place to hold information that you may need soon or that you have not yet filed away. The proper name for this memory is Random Access Memory (RAM), and as the name implies, it can be accessed as needed by the CPU and could also be considered a short term parking lot on the motherboard highway system.

The longer term parking (or file cabinet) inside your computer would be your hard drive. The hard drive is where you would keep information (data) and instructions (software) that you are not currently using. To some extent, you have control over how things are filed on your hard drive and to some extent you do not. In other words, the "system", for now let's just say the CPU, makes many filing decisions based on the speed of recovery and the frequency of use. A good example of this would be your "boot" files. These are files that the computer uses every time that it starts up (boots) so they are filed in what is known as the boot sector, which is at the front of the filing system. Later we will look at the files that you have control over and how to keep them organized in a way that you will be able to find them when you need them.

Up until now we have been talking about a single computer, but what if you were to hook this computer to another computer and then hook that one to yet another? This is what is commonly known as a network. If you then hook this network to another network and repeat this several times you will end up with the internet. As the information comes and goes through your computer it needs a way in and out. Similar to the onramp of our information highway (or the front door to your house), the computer has a pathway and it is called the network card (NIC). The network card is the place where the wire that carries all of the external information plugs into your computer.

To review:

- **Motherboard = Highway System**

- **CPU = Brain**

- **Memory (RAM) = Short Term Parking or Inbox/Outbox**

- **Hard Drive = Long Term Parking or File Cabinet**

- **Network Card = Onramp or Front Door**

For now these are the important parts inside your computer that you should know. The truth is that the inside of the computer is much more complex and would take years to fully understand, but for the everyday user, a simple understanding of the internal workings will help you to know what you can do to work with the computer and not fight it in your day to day life. At the end of this book you will find a glossary of common computer terms and their definitions to help you along. Hopefully, by the end of this book you will have the ability to use the internet to do further research.

What are the Different Types of Computers?

There are many types of computers, but **personal computers** such as **desktop** and **laptop** computers are probably the two types of computers that you think of first.

- Desktop Computers or Towers

    - Case containing the main components

    - Monitor

    - Keyboard

    - Mouse

*The term **desktop computer** originated when the computer case was wide and flat, and was designed specifically to **fit on your desktop** with the monitor on top of it.

Figure 2

*Tower Computers are sometimes called desktops, but they more commonly set beside or under the desk and stand vertical like a tower.

Figure 3

Figure 4

Laptop Computers

Laptop (notebook, netbook, portable) computers have a battery and are much smaller and more portable. Due to the size, it is more difficult to upgrade and will run hotter than most desktop units.

The obvious advantage to the laptop is its portability.

*   *Heat is a major enemy to a computer. Heat will slow the processing speed and could cause damage to internal parts. Most modern computers will automatically shut down if they get too hot to protect internal parts.*

Types of Personal Computers

Two popular types of personal computers are the **IBM compatible** and **Macintosh** computers. The first personal computer was produced by IBM in 1981 and was called the **IBM PC**. In 1984, Apple Computer introduced the Macintosh, or **Mac**, and it became the first widely sold personal computer with a graphical user interface or GUI (pronounced goo-ee). Although both IBM and Apple computers are personal computers, the term PC came to refer to IBM or IBM-compatible personal computers.

Apple produced a Macintosh computer called the **iMac**, which is a desktop computer that features an **all-in-one design**. This means all the internal components are located behind the monitor, rather than in a tower case, which was a custom design in desktop computers. Other manufacturers have followed suit and now you can get PC computers in the all-in-one design.

While our training is intended for people who use PCs and the Windows operating system, some of our information also applies to Macintosh computers.

You may hear someone refer to a computer as a **workstation** or a **server**, especially at work. You may wonder how these two items are different from desktop computers.

Workstations are similar to desktop computers, but are more powerful and are usually connected to a network. **Servers** are specialized computers that store and deliver, or "serve up," information to other computers on a network.

There are many different types of servers such as **file servers**, **database servers**, and **web servers**. For example, employees at a company might store all the business documents on a **file server** so that they can share files and access them from any computer on the network. When you use your browser to click a link, a **web server** delivers the page you requested on the Internet, the biggest network in the world.

Setting up the computer

What are all the buttons, sockets and slots used for?

- The Basic Parts to a Desktop Computer

    – External

        • Computer case

        • Monitor

        • Keyboard

        • Mouse

        • Power cord

        • Other optional add ons

    – Internal (All-In-One Computers occasionally integrate some of these components)

        • Front of the Case

            – Power Button

            – CD ROM and/or DVD ROM (or blu-ray)

                • Reader/writer

            – USB port

            – Audio In/Audio Out

- Back of the Case

    - 1. PS/2 Port

    - 2. Ethernet Port

    - 3. Audio In/Audio Out

    - 4. VGA Port (DVI)

    - 5. USB Port

Figure 5

- Back of the Case

    - 1. Parallel Port

    - 2. Serial Port

    - 3. Expansion Slots

    - FireWire Port

Figure 6

9

It is important to know that in almost all cases, the only wire that will fit into the port on the computer is the correct wire. In some cases you will have to be careful and make sure that you are pushing the connector in straight and not twisting it, but as a rule, if it fits, it is correct. Simply position the computer where you can see the ports, look at the wire and plug it in where it fits. As you can see above, there is usually more than one USB port. You will find that many different components can connect to these ports. Don't be concerned if you do not find anything to plug into all ports. You will have some that are not used. For example, most new keyboards and mice will use a USB connector whereas the older ones used the PS/2 connector. Another thing you will notice is that there are USB ports (and possibly some others) on both the front and back of your computer. This is not a problem, simply use the one that works best for you. Remember, if you connect a camera, a phone, a flash drive or any other add-on later, it will be more convenient to use the front ports so try to use the rear ports for things that will remain plugged in most of the time.

When everything else is connected, you can plug in the power cord. It is VERY important that you use a surge protector and keep in mind that not all power strips are surge protectors. If it is a surge protector, it will say so on the package. If you do not have a package, you should see an indicator light on the strip that will illuminate when you are protected. If you do not see a light, get a new surge protector. Surge protection is very inexpensive compared to the cost of a new computer. If that is all that you have to be concerned with, it is worth the investment. Considering that if you were to get a power surge you could potentially lose all of your data stored on that computer, protection is something you should never be without.

When choosing a surge protector, you do not have to spend a lot of money to get good protection. Most packaging will give you three different ratings that you should consider. First you should look for clamping voltage. This will tell you how much voltage can leak through before the unit will shut it down. The number to look for is less than 400v. Next you should look for the energy absorption/dissipation rating. This will be given in joules and you should look for 600 joules or more. The last rating is the response time and less than 1 nanosecond is preferable. Also, you should always choose a protector that has an indicator light on it. Even the best protector will stop protecting after a certain number of surges and without an indicator light, you will never know if that limit has been reached. You will find that many companies will offer free insurance for your hardware and software. This is a good indicator that the surge protector is good and even if it does not protect your computer, the manufacturer may cover it.

Software

Software is any set of instructions that tells the hardware what to do. Often referred to as programs, software is the key to converting your computer from a worthless piece of electronic parts to a productive, fun, entertaining and functioning piece of equipment. When you load a program on your computer, you are giving it a set of instructions.

Let's look at it in a different way. In the early days of electronic computers, an operator would type a command on his/her keyboard and the computer would perform an action. If the operator wanted to add 2 + 2, he would have to type something like this:

"Add the number '2' to the number '2' and display the result on the screen."

As you can see, this limits the productivity of the computer. Later "programmers", a new type of operators, found a way to store common tasks and activate them as needed, saving the operator from having to input them every time. This stored task is known as a command and combining many commands together is called a program. Below is a set of commands combined into a simple program.

1. Input #1

2. Input #2

3. Input #3

4. If #2 = "+", then add #1 and #3

5. If #2 = "*", then multiply #1 by #3

6. If #2 = "/", then divide #1 by #3

7. If #2 = "-", then subtract #3 from #1

8. Show result on the screen

First the program waits for user input, #1. Second it waits for input #2. Third it waits for input #3. Now with the information provided by the user, the program knows what to do.

If the user input "156 * 894", then the computer would understand 156 would need to be multiplied by 894 and the output on the screen would read 139,464.

As you can see, if an operator wanted to manipulate numbers all day long, it would become quite cumbersome to input the entire program every time. By saving the program and calling it up as needed, the user becomes much more productive. As you may have figured out, this program is what is called up every time you turn on the most basic pocket calculator. By now a light bulb may have lit up above your head and you realized that a calculator is none other than a simple computer.

Today's programs have thousands of commands written into them. Each command can be controlled by a user's (operator's) input, or it can be activated by a previous command. The line in the above program telling the computer to show the result on the screen is an example of a command activated by a previous command. When the user is finished inputting the three instructions that are being asked for, the program performs the task and displays the output. Think of some of the programs used today and how many commands have to be built into them. Today's calculators do much more than adding two numbers together. Take for example the simple formula Pi times the radius squared used to find the area of a circle. Today's calculators require you to provide the radius and the rest is in the program saving you a lot of input.

You may be thinking, "With the size and power of today's programs, what keeps them from interfering with each other?" Good question. Today we can run many programs all at the same time. We might be typing an e-mail while surfing the web and playing a game. So what keeps this all straight? The operating system is in charge.

The Operating System

The main software that is in charge of the computer is the Operating System (OS). An Operating System is the most important software that runs on a computer. The operating system performs many essential tasks for your computer. It controls the memory needed for computer processes, manages disk space, controls peripheral devices, and allows you to communicate with the computer without knowing exactly how a computer works. Without an operating system, a computer is useless.

The truth is that there are many operating systems available today. Most of these OS's are very specialized, and according to Net Applications.com, adding them all up they comprise less than 2% of the market share (as of November 2010). The top 4 OS's comprise an impressive 98.13% of the market with the top seller, Windows making up 90.81%. Apple's Mac operating system is number 2 and currently it controls only 5.03%, with their iOS (also known as the iPhone OS) in third place with 1.36% shares. The other one worth mentioning is the Linux OS with just under 1%. For obvious reasons, we will spend most of our time discussing Microsoft's Windows OS and other software operating on a Windows-based system.

Popular Operating Systems

1. Windows

    o   Windows 7

    o   Windows Vista

    o   Windows XP

    o   Windows ME/Windows Millennium or 2000

    o   Windows 98

    o   Windows 95 and so on

2. Apple OS

    o   IOS

3. Linux

In a PC, there is one piece of software that operates first when you turn your computer on just prior to the Operating System taking over. That is the BIOS or basic input/output system. Its main job is to locate your hardware, then locate the operating system and then turn the computer over so the OS can do its job. The BIOS is hard coded into the computer, which simply means that it will remain ready to do its job even if you have no hard drive installed and the computer has been unplugged. Once the computer is up and running, the BIOS serves no purpose.

Now that we have covered the bases and talked about the BIOS and other operating systems, we can focus on Microsoft Windows. In fact, we will talk some about Windows XP, a little about Windows Vista, but our main focus will be on Windows 7.

Windows

Windows XP was introduced in 2001 as a replacement for the aging 9X series including Windows 95 and

Windows 98. Through the years Microsoft updated this operating system using three major "service

packs." Service pack 3, introduced in April 2008, is currently the only version of this OS that is still being

supported by Microsoft with updates and fixes to any security issues. This support is scheduled to be

discontinued in April 2014, but with the changes that have been included in the Windows 7 OS; most

users will retire XP long before the support ends. Anyone currently running anything prior to XP SP3 is

risking infection and theft of personal information through malware, which will be discussed later in this

book.

Windows Vista was released in November of 2006 to business customers and then in January 2007 to

the general public. The main changes from prior versions included an enhanced security and a more

user- friendly layout. Vista was met with a lot of criticism and quickly was found to have many security

issues. Microsoft worked hard to fix the problems with patches, but by late 2009, less than 3 years after

the release of Vista, Microsoft introduced Windows 7.

In the short time that Windows 7 has been in use it has proven to be everything that was promised and

much more, outselling every other operating system in history. Learning from the problems in Vista and

listening to user feedback, Microsoft developed a user-friendly, secure, and highly functional OS.

The modern operating system is much more than just an operating system. Features and other

programs are built into the operating system to add to the user experience. For example, an operating

system can function and do everything that it needs to do without having a fancy desktop or a built-in calculator. There is no need to include a word processor or games, but they are included. When we talk about an operating system today, we talk about the entire package much in the way we look at a new car. The car will do its job getting you from place to place without having power windows or air conditioning. The truth is, you don't NEED a windshield for a car to do its job, but you probably would not buy a car if these things were left out. The same is true with an operating system. The job of the OS is simply to act as an interface for the user to communicate with the hardware and other software, but they have become so much more.

*   It is worth noting that each new version of the operating system makes strides in not only ease of use but also in security and power consumption.

*   The latest OS from Microsoft, Windows 7 has made huge advances, and if you are currently running an older OS you may want to consider upgrading.

Getting Started

Now that we have looked at the computer hardware and the software it is time to put them both together. In other words, it's time to power up your computer and go hands on. First we need to check and review some points.

- ➢ If you are using a laptop on battery power, make sure that your battery is charged. If not, plug in your power cord.
- ➢ If you are on a desktop or tower make sure that you are plugged into an acceptable surge protector.

The power button will have some variation of the symbol in figure 7 on it. Some are colored, some are lit, and some are hidden in places you would never think to look. I

Figure 7

have seen the power button on a laptop placed in the end of the hinge for the monitor, some are on the side, and still others are next to the keyboard. On a tower, some are behind a door, but most are on the front. One thing to keep in mind on a desktop or tower is that most power supplies, even though they are built in, have a separate power switch. This switch is located on the back of the computer and "on" is indicated by a straight line (|) and off will be a circle (O). This switch can be left on almost all the time and is only turned off if you are opening the computer case for service. Another thing to remember is that the surge protector should have a power switch and this will need to remain on. Your monitor will also have its own power switch. Make sure all of the switches are on and only then press the main power button.

The first this thing you will see is a black screen with white information scrolling by. This is the BIOS going through its system checks. At some point it will pause for a short time and will tell you that if you would like to go to setup you should press some key. You can ignore this and let it pass. Next, your operating system will take over. We are going to be talking about Windows 7 from this point forward, but if you are using a different OS, things will be similar.

Once the boot process is complete you will be looking at a login screen. This screen (seen in figure 8), depending on the number of users on your computer, could have one or more user names and passwords. On your initial boot of the computer you will be asked to set up users and you will be able to change them anytime. You also have the option to not set up users, but this is not recommended for security reasons that we will discuss later. We will also be discussing proper passwords later, but for now set up a password that you can remember and is not a name, address, phone number or any other easy to find number, name or word. Passwords are case sensitive so remember how you type it. Do not forget your password.

* If the computer was set up without a password you will not see the login screen and will be taken directly to the desktop.

Figure 8

Navigation

What good is your computer if you can't get where you want to go? It is pretty to look at and makes a nice nightlight, but that is about it. The key to being able to get the most out of your computer is to be able to get around in the most comfortable and efficient way. Windows offers a lot of flexibility in this.

In most cases, there are at least 3 ways to do anything in Windows. This is sometimes a good thing, but often, for the novice, this can be very confusing. As we go through this chapter, I will try to give you one main way to do something and follow up with some alternatives. This is not to say that the main way, or even my favorite way, is the best way, but rather that if you learn one way and have trouble executing it, you almost always have an alternative. In the back of the book in appendix 1 is a list of the most common tasks and some of the ways to execute them. This list is in no way all inclusive and some readers will discover new methods of performing tasks that work better for them. This is not only fine, but is encouraged. By far, the most rewarding part of learning the computer basics is discovering new things. Experimenting and exploring, well let's just say it, playing around is encouraged. Not to say that it cannot happen, but (as long as your work is saved) it is very rare that you can do any damage that cannot be undone. Have fun!

The Desktop

When you first start your computer you will see a screen that could be solid color, have a logo, or even a picture. This is what is called the desktop. The desktop is your home base and is where you will want to be when you are starting your navigation. You will also see a group of small pictures that are labeled with names. These are called icons. Looking around you can see the Start or Windows Button, the Task Bar and more icons in the task bar.

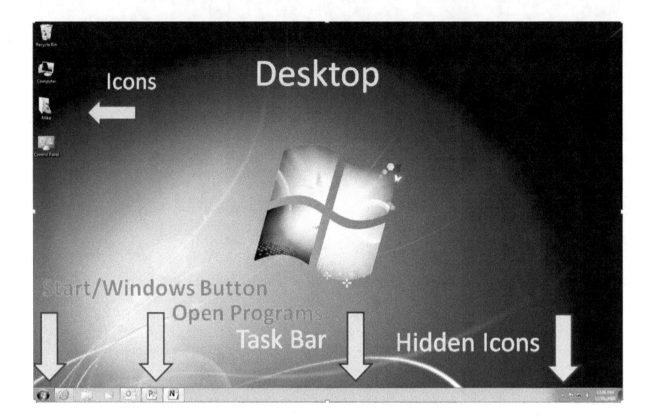

Figure 9

In the lower right corner you will see the date and time, some other small icons and an up arrow. At this point, it is only important that you know these names, not so much what each one does. Mark this page and come back to it often.

> * If you do not see the task bar on your desktop, drag your mouse down to the bottom of the screen and it should pop up. This can be adjusted by right clicking on the task bar and selecting properties.

The Mouse

In 1984, Apple introduced the Macintosh and it came with a new navigation device called the mouse. It was easy to see where it got its name. It was a palm sized unit with a long tail-like cord out one end. It truly looked like a mouse. Over the years, inventing a better mouse has become similar to trying to come up with a better mouse trap. Out of all of the different configurations of mice, there are three things they all have in common; the tracker, left button, and right button. Other buttons, rollers and even fancy designs are available today. In fact, you can get a mouse that looks just like a mouse. For the purpose of this lesson, we will stick with the basics. Keep in mind that, if you are left handed, the left and right mouse buttons can be switched for convenience so as we go through this chapter, if I say click the left mouse button and you have them switched, just do the opposite.

The Tracker

In the old days, and we are talking computers so the old days could be last week, a mouse had what was called a roller ball. Most modern mice have what is called an optical tracker or a laser. Whatever they have, the job is the same, to control the position of the cursor on the screen.

1. Position the mouse in your right hand so that your palm is resting on the back of the mouse and your index finger is on the left button.

    a. Play with it now.

    b. Move it across the desk and watch the cursor moving on the screen. It takes some time to get smooth operation out of it, but try moving the cursor from one corner of the screen to another.

2. Now for fun, turn your mouse over so the buttons are under the heel of your hand and try to move from the upper left to the lower right side of your screen.

    a. If you have some experience and you can navigate smoothly, this little experiment demonstrates how many beginners feel.

3. Turn it back to the proper position.

    a. Take your time, watch the cursor and move your hand. The more that you do it, the easier it will get.

4. Position your cursor over the Recycle Bin. (If you do not have a recycle bin showing, use any icon.)

5. Pick up your mouse and move it to a different location.

    a. Notice that the cursor remains where it was.

    b. Remember this little trick if you happen to get to the edge of your desk and need to continue. Simply pick up the mouse and move it back onto the desk.

The Buttons

To use a mouse, you click it. You can single click, double click or hold a mouse button. If someone tells you to click, or if this book tells you to click, it always means a single left click, unless otherwise specified. If ever you need to double click or right click, you will be told to do so. With that said, here comes one of the confusing alternatives that Windows offers. There are settings in the OS that allow you to change a double click required function into a single click. If you have a computer that is set this way, never fear. Whatever way you do it will become second nature to you and you soon will be doing it without even thinking.

The Left Mouse Button

The left button is by far the most used of all of the mouse controls. It is used to select, drag, open, and in combination with keyboard keys, select multiples. Let's try selecting first.

1. Remember placing your cursor over the recycle bin in the last paragraph? Try it one more time.

    a. Notice that the Icon is highlighted.

    b. Now move the mouse and the cursor away and notice that the icon is back to normal.

c. Move it back and click the left mouse button one time and move the cursor away again. This time the icon remains highlighted. This is referred to as "selecting" the icon.

2. Now, with that icon selected, move down a few icons and hover (move the cursor over and leave it there) over it.

   a. As you can see, this icon is also highlighted. Now click one time. Notice that the recycle bin icon is no longer highlighted.

3. This time, leaving the second icon highlighted, hover over the recycle bin one more time.

   a. On your keyboard press and hold the shift key then click the left mouse button and release both. Notice that this time every icon from the first click to the second click is highlighted.

4. Click somewhere on the desktop where there are no icons.

   a. Notice now that nothing is highlighted.

5. Click on the Recycle bin one time.

   a. Now move to another icon leaving at least one in between.

   b. Hold down the Control (Ctrl) key and then click. You should now see only the two icons selected.

   c. Now move to another icon, hold the Crtl key and click this icon. Now you should see three icons selected. This can be repeated as many times as needed.

Now try your double click skills.

1. Move your cursor over the recycle bin and double click it.

   a. Double clicking is two quick clicks on the left mouse button. If done correctly you should see a window open and in the top (address bar) of the window it should say "Recycle Bin."

You just opened a window. If this was an icon for a program, double clicking would have opened or started the program. In an open window you will see in the upper right hand corner one of two groups of buttons. If the window is shrunk or a partial screen, you will see . If the window is full screen you will see Notice that the only difference is that the middle button is a single square, which clicked will make this window the only one visible (full screen) or a double square tell you that clicking this will shrink the window so you can see others behind it. The left button, the minus sign, will minimize your window, which means that it will only show as an icon in the task bar. To get it back you can click on its icon in the task bar and it will return to the screen. Notice that in Windows 7 you can hover over the icons and see a preview of the open window. This comes in handy when you have multiple incidences of a folder or program open and you only want to see one of them.

When your window is partial screen, you can move your cursor to the top bar to the left of the buttons, click and hold your left mouse button, and drag the window to the position you want. Careful, in Windows 7 a feature called window snap has been added. If you drag your window to the top of the screen and the cursor touches the top, your window will snap to full screen. Also, if you drag it to the left or the right side it will snap to half screen.

Another way to use the drag feature is to grab an icon, file or folder and move it.

1. Try grabbing the Recycle bin and moving it to the middle of your desktop and dropping it. (Some of you will notice that the rest of the icons jumped into the void left where the recycle bin was. This is because of a setting that auto arranges the icons on the desktop.)
2. Now move it back to where it was.
   a. Be very careful not to drop it into a folder or on top of another icon. This will move it inside of that folder. In fact, if you drop a file on top of the recycle bin you will have

done the same as deleting the file. To avoid this you need to watch the icons around the place that you wish to drop and make sure that they are not highlighted (lit up.)

We have not yet tried clicking on the big red X in the upper right corner, but I think you can guess what will happen. Yes, it closes the open window. Now you can select one or more, open, minimize, maximize, drag, snap, and close using one button.

The Right Mouse Button

The right button is often called the menu button.

1. Move your curser to an open place on your computer desktop and click the right button. As you can see, a menu pops up.

2. Now left click on the desktop and it goes away.

3. Move to the task bar and right click. A different menu pops up.

4. Hover over the recycle bin and right click.

As you can see, right click is a very powerful tool. Wherever you use it, you get a new group of options. As you learn more you will see that this button will help you out in many situations. Try it any time you do not see what you are looking for and you may find it.

The Scroll Wheel

Most new mice have a wheel located between the left and right buttons that is called the scroll wheel. You will find that if a window has too much to be displayed in your screen there will be a scroll bar on the side of the screen to navigate up and down. The scroll wheel will do the same thing without moving your hand. Simply move your index finger to the wheel and roll it and the window will move up and down. Some scroll wheels can also be clicked, which activates a zoom option where rolling it one way

zooms in and the other way zooms out.

> I would highly recommend at this time that you play around. Click on things, right click on

  things, open things and close them. For additional mouse exercises visit the web site

  http://www.instruction.greenriver.edu/avery/activities/mouse/MouseSkills.htm and go through

  the step as often as it takes till you feel comfortable.

The Touchpad

Most laptop computers have a built in touchpad as a substitution for a mouse. The touchpad serves the

same functions as the mouse but instead of moving it across your desk you simply place one finger on

the pad and move it around. It takes some practice but you can navigate the screen, click left and right,

and drag just like the mouse. Some touchpads have a pinch feature where you can place two fingers on

the pad and move them together and zoom in and out on the window similar to one of the scroll wheel

features.

The Keyboard

Keyboards, like mice are available in many styles. Also like mice, the basic parts or keys on the keyboard

are fairly standard throughout the industry. Some have 85 keys, some have 104, and still others have

more, but the basic letters and numbers are in the same location on most of them. It is interesting to

know that the layout of the keys was first designed in the late 1800's and was done to make typing as

difficult as possible. It seems that the first typewriters had a problem. The arms that hit the paper when

the keys were depressed would catch on each other and stick if they did not have time to return before the next one advanced to the paper. This problem was worse if the letters were next to each other. To fix this problem, a key layout was used that spread the most common used letters out and made fast typing difficult. The problem was solved. Today the original problem is not an issue, yet with all the attempts that have been made over the years to rearrange the keys, all have failed because people are used to the current layout.

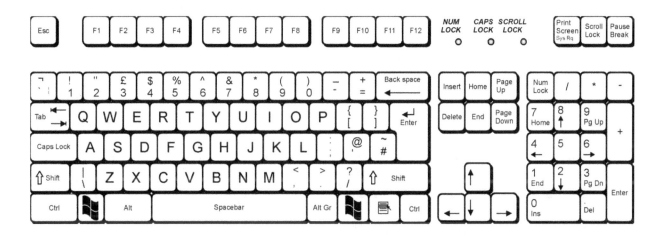

Figure 10

The most common computer keyboards used today have 85 or 104 keys. You have 26 letter keys, 10 number keys, the basic tab, shift, space and so on, then a row of "f" keys. In addition, many computer keyboards offer a set of number keys to the right side for quick number entry. Some keys of interest are the "Windows" keys (pointed out in figure 11 with the blue arrows) and the "menu" key (pointed out with the yellow arrow).

Not always in the same place and not always two of them, the Windows keys serve a very specialized function. Wherever you are and whatever screen you are in, press the Windows key and you will see your start menu. It is also interesting to note that the button that you click on the screen to get the same menu also has the same design and is in the lower left corner. Another key that is not always there and sometimes in a different location is the "menu" key which functions just like the right mouse button; it opens a menu for your current location.

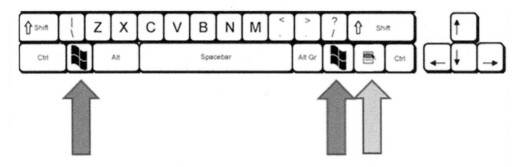

Figure 11

Navigation keys, the arrow keys, Home, End, page up and down, often can be used in place of moving the mouse. Above the top row of number keys you will see many special characters that can be accessed by holding the shift key. Most commonly on laptop computers but sometimes on desktops, you will see a blue symbol on the keys. These functions are accessed by holding a "Mode" key and it is often located in the lower left, but can be anywhere on the keyboard.

On the top side of your keyboard you will find the "F" or function keys. These keys are very flexible, and depending where you are and which programs are open, the "F" may perform very different functions. For example, if you are at your desktop with nothing open and you press Alt + Ctrl + F2, a new Word document opens. Of course if you do not have Microsoft Office loaded on your computer, this function will not work the same way. The secret is to try them and see what they do. The only constant is the F1 key, and it also has some exceptions. F1 is almost always your "help" key. If nothing is open, F1 will give you general windows help. If you are in a Word document, F1 will give you Word help and so on. Wherever you are, F1 is your answer key.

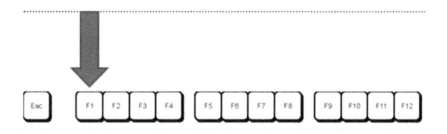

Figure 12

Most of the other keys are self-explanatory except possibly the Caps Lock and the Num Lock. The Caps Lock, when pressed one time, is the same as holding the shift key when typing letters. This will become very important later on when we talk about passwords. Many keyboards have an indicator light that tells you if Caps Lock is on. Summarily the Num Lock locks the number keys on the right side of the keyboard so they operate as numbers. To unlock the Caps Lock and the Num Lock, simply press again. If you will notice, the number keys also have arrows, Home, End and other functions if the Num Lock is not on.

Take some time and experiment with your keyboard and learn how it works. There are many more "secret" functions or "shortcuts" that can be performed with different key combinations, but this is not the place to cover them. If you are interested, I have included many shortcuts in the Appendix at the end of this book.

Touchscreen

Touchscreen technology has come and gone through the years. It has its place on specialized computers and on phones and GPS units, but it seems that on the standard home or workplace computer, people like the feel of the keyboard and mouse. Touchscreen allows the user to interact directly with the screen by touching, tapping, dragging and so on. This technology is very individualized and as you come across it, you will need to try it, touch it, feel it and learn it.

Starting a Program

In Windows 7 Microsoft made some nice changes which made finding and opening programs much easier. All of the older methods still apply, so we will go through a few different ways starting with the newest. Remember the start or Windows button we discussed when we looked at the desktop? In the lower left corner of your screen on the task bar you will find it. Remember it, use it, become friends with it. It will come in handy quite often.

In the following demonstrations we will be opening the "Internet Explorer" program. With some slight and obvious changes you should be able to open any program.

Method 1:

1. Click on the Windows/start button

2. Notice that you have a blinking curser in the box labeled "Search programs and files." Begin typing the program name "Internet Explorer" but stop at "Int" You will see that a menu pops up and at the top is the Internet Explorer program.

Figure 13

3. Click on the word Internet Explorer and your Internet Explorer will open.

Remember that to close a program you can click on the red X in the top right corner.

Method 2 (if you know where the program is found):

1. Click on the Windows/start button

2. Two lines up you will see a right arrow and the words "all Programs." Hover over this.

3. In the new menu scroll down to the program Internet Explorer and click on it.

Method 3 (this may not work on all computers and will NOT work for all programs):

1. Look at your desktop and locate the Internet Explorer icon.

2. Double click on it.

Method 4 (again this may not work on all computers and will NOT work on some):

1. Look at your task bar and locate the Internet Explorer icon

2. Click on it

As you can see, some methods take a few more steps, some take a little searching, still others may not work on the program you are looking for, but the end result of each method is the same. Another thing to remember is that you can sometimes open more than one instance of the same program. I am sure that this has happened to some people as you followed along. This is not a problem and you can close each one with the red X in the upper right corner. Sometimes you will want to have more than one program open and need to navigate between them. Alt + Tab in combination is an easy way to do this.

In method 3 and 4 we are relying on the fact that the program is "pinned" to the start menu or the task bar. In Windows 7 you have the option to pin or unpin your most used programs and files so these methods will work for you. Pinning and unpinning it done by right clicking on the icon.

Opening a File

A computer file is actually a block of arbitrary information saved to a storage device. This means that a program its self is stored as files. That said, for the purposes of this book we will consider files as documents, pictures, or any other viewable thing that you create and store.

Opening files is much the same as opening programs. In fact, to open a file you will actually open the program that will display that file. So in a way this is just one more method to open a program. For example, if you would like to open a picture that you have stored on your computer's hard drive and you know the name of the file, you can use the same steps in method 1 above, replacing the program name with the file name. Let's assume your picture is called Desert.

1. Click on the Windows/start button

2. Notice that you have a blinking curser in the box

Figure 13

   labeled "Search programs and files." Begin typing the picture name "Desert" but stop at "Des." You will see that a menu pops up. As you look down the list you will see a header called Pictures. Under this header you will see Desert.

3. Click on the word Desert and your Picture will open.

Methods 2 above will also work with files as will method 3 if the file happens to be stored on the desktop.

But wait, what actually opens was Windows Picture Viewer and the Desert picture is in the program. That is right; files depend on programs to display them. The same is true for documents, pictures, spreadsheets, or anything else. Also, some files can be opened and displayed by more than one program. Let's try a little twist on method 1.

1. Click on the Windows/start button

2. Notice that you have a blinking curser in the box labeled "Search programs and files." Begin typing the

32   **Figure 14**

picture name "Desert" but stop at "Des." You will see that a menu pops up. As you look down the list you will see a header called Pictures. Under this header you will see Desert.

3. This time right click on Desert.

4. Select "open with"

5. In the list choose "Paint"

Now you are viewing the same picture file, but this time the program you are using is Paint. Now that paint is open, let's try a new method for opening files.

In the upper left corner of Paint you will see one or two down arrows. We are interested in the one that you see shaded blue with the menu symbol to the left of it.

Figure 15

1. Click on this arrow.

2. Select "open" by clicking on it.

3. In the pop up window, locate a file called "Lighthouse." This can be done several ways, but the simplest, sense we know the name, would be to type the name in the search space at the top right corner.

4. Highlight the file by clicking once on it. Notice that the file name appears at the bottom of the window next to "File name:"

5. Click on "Open"

You can use any means that suits your needs and preference to open files. As I said before, the end result is the same no matter how you do it. The key is to know some different options so that, if you do not know where the file is stored, you can search for it and if you are not sure of the name, you can look for it.

Saving a file

Saving files is very important and should be done often. Until a file is saved it only exists in the

computers RAM and if you remember from reading chapter 1, RAM is only temporary storage. If you

were to close a program or power down the computer, either intentionally or accidentally, prior to

saving the job you are working on, all of your work will be lost. Save early and save often for your

protection.

Open the program "WordPad." Don't tell me you forgot how to do that? It was just in the last

paragraph.

1.   Click on the Windows/start button.

2.   In the search box begin typing "WordPad."

3.   When you see the program appear in the menu, click on it.

Now you have a blank document in front of you and you can start typing your note. This is the point you

should first save your document. You may be saying to yourself, "why save it now, there is nothing on

it?" That may be true, but consider this. Your file is not currently named. You have not chosen a

location that you would like to save to. If you start typing and get into your work and all of a sudden you

get called away so you close the program. Better yet the worst happens and you have a power outage.

Can you think of some of the words that you may use when you realize you just lost your work?

Now let's look at the other option. When you first open a document, spreadsheet, or whatever you are

working on, you should save it. Name it, select a location, and save it. Why? Because many programs

will auto save every so often while you are working. If you have a name and location chosen, you are

more likely to recover at least some of your work if the worst happens. Another reason now is the time you are thinking about what you are doing. You know what you are going to name it and where you will store it. If you are like me right now, I am thinking about this book and what the next line needs to be and I do not want to stop and think about a document name and where to save it, I just want to save it and move on.

The actual process of saving is simple and like all things Windows, you can do it many different ways.

1. The top left of most programs you will see the word "file" or a down arrow. Click on either and select "save" or "save as" from the menu.

2. The first time you save a project (or if you click "save as") you will get a pop up window asking you to name your project and select a location to save to. We will get into naming and filing methods in the next chapter so for now call your file "Note"

3. Select the location as "Desktop"

4. Click the "Save" button.

Now that you have a name and location saving becomes very simple.

1. Click on "file"

2. Click on "save"

Or you can…

1. Click on the save logo that looks like this.

Or you can…

1. While holding the Ctrl key, press the letter "S"

Some programs have other ways of saving but these are the basics.

If you click on "save" or "save as" you may notice that the default folder is "My Documents." There is a reason for this. It is arguably the best place to save your files, at least for short term. Some people will tell you to save to the desktop, but to me this is the same as receiving a letter in the mail and throwing it down on your desk. You know you will sooner or later have to deal with it so why not do it now and save some work. Let me explain my reasoning.

For many years, Microsoft has created a default folder for each user called "My Documents" and now in Vista and 7 it is called just "Documents." This is the folder that is listed when you save documents and it is the easiest folder to get to when looking for a file. In fact, while in a program if you were to click "open" you are first taken to this folder to look for your file. In Windows 7, the Documents feature is actually a virtual library. You do not need to know what that means, but just knowing that Microsoft planned it and they have thousands of experts working for them should be enough. It just works. Files are easier to find, easier to back up, and easier to keep separate from programs thus protecting them from accidental deletion during program updates.

Next you should develop or adopt a consistent method for naming files. For example, if you have clients you may want to name your files with the client name followed by the 6 digit date. Smith,T101511 would be the name of a file that you saved for Tom Smith on October 15, 2011. Using this method, the standard alphanumeric sort will display your client files grouped by name and arranged by date. Perhaps you are a student and you would like to save your files by semester and class and date. Whatever method suited your needs and will allow you to find the file as needed is the one you should use. The trick is to stick with it.

Another clue to good filing is to keep the name short. Even though Windows will allow you to use long file names, this is seldom the best practice. You want to be able to quickly scan through file names when you are looking for a file and if the names are long this will take a substantial amount of time. In fact, consider using abbreviations.

Let your folder structure take some of the sorting burden. Consider folders as you would in a file cabinet. You can place single folders in the drawer, or you can place a large folder (or tab) in and then place many folders inside that folder. This works well if you started off thinking that you would only have a few files and later you would only have a few files and later

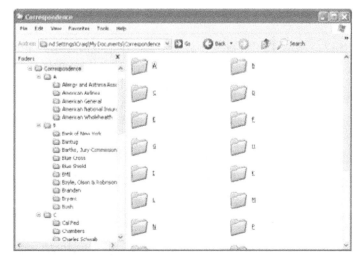

Figure 16

found that you have many. In the client example earlier you may need to give each client their own folder. After you are in business for a while you may find that even this is quite cumbersome so you may need to separate in groups like the first letter of the last name so you can create folders as seen in the illustration. Simply dragging and dropping the existing folder into the new folder as needed will do the trick. How do I do that? Keep reading.

Organizing files

Now that you have saved some files you may have decided that you need to change some names or move them to a different location. This is a simple process in Windows.

Renaming a File

1. Open the folder that contains the file that you would like to rename. Assuming that this is the "Documents" folder you can open it by double clicking on the desktop shortcut, if you have one, or by clicking the start button, then clicking on the word "documents."

2. Now find the file that you wish to rename and right click on it.

3. You will see a menu pop up and in the menu, click on the word "Rename."

4. Notice that your file name is highlighted blue. At this point you can simply type the new name and hit the enter key. Now, you will see the new file name.

An alternative to this process is as follows.

1. Open the folder that contains the file that you would like to rename. Assuming that this is the "Documents" folder you can open it by double clicking on the desktop shortcut, if you have one, or by clicking the start button, then clicking on the word "documents."

2. Now find the file that you wish to rename and left click on it one time to select it.

3. On the top bar you wills see the word "Organize" with a down arrow, click on it.

4. In the drop down menu click on "Rename."

5. Notice that your file name is highlighted blue. At this point you can simply type the new name and hit the enter key. Now, you will see the new file name.

Making a New Folder

We will assume your folder is still open. If not, follow step one above.

1. On the top bar you will see the words "New folder," click on them.

2. In your list of files and folders you will see a new folder appear and it will be named "New Folder."

3. Notice that the name is highlighted in blue. Type your new folder name and hit the enter key.

An Alternative method is as follows.

1. In a blank area inside the folder right click.

2. In the pop up menu hover over the word "New."

3. Move your pointer over to the word "Folder" and click.

4. In your list of files and folders you will see a new folder appear and it will be named "New Folder."

5. Notice that the name is highlighted in blue. Type your new folder name and hit the enter key.

Moving Files and Folders

Remember from the chapter on navigation that we discussed dragging and dropping? This is a simple way of moving files and folders. Again we will assume your folder is still open. First we will need to have a file and some folders to move.

1. Make a new folder and name it "New folder 1."

2. Make a new folder and name it "New folder 2."

3. Make a new document file and name it "New document file 1."

    a. Do this by right clicking on blank spot inside the folder.

    b. Hover over the word "New"

    c. Move your pointer to the words "Text Document" and click.

    d. Type the new name.

  e. Hit the enter key

4. Make a new document file and name it "New document file 2."

Now that we have some folders and files to work with let's do same arranging. First place "New document 1" inside "New folder 1."

1. Grab "New document file 1" with a left mouse click.

2. Holding the left mouse button, drag the file over "New folder 1" till you see it highlighted.

3. Drop the file by letting go of the mouse button.

Follow the same steps and move "New document file 2" into "New folder 2."

Now you can no longer see the files in your current folder. You can check to be sure they are in the new folders by right clicking on the folders and in the pop up menu click on "Open in new window." Can you see it? Now close "New folder 2" and leave "New folder 1" open. Remember the red X. Now resize the document folder and the new folder 1 to half screen so that you can see them both. If you are using Windows 7 this is done simply by dragging the folder (grab the top bar) to the side of the screen till your mouse pointer touches the edge and letting go. This is the snap feature in Windows 7. Do the same with the other folder except take it to the other side. If you are not in Windows 7 you will need to do the following.

1. In the upper right make sure you see a single box between the _ and the X.

  a. If you see a double box, click on it.

2. Now drag the window to the top right corner of your screen.

3. Move you pointer to the left edge of the window till it turns into a double arrow.

4. Hold the left mouse button and drag the edge to the approximate middle of the screen and drop it.

5. Move your pointer the bottom edge of the window and do the same, dragging it to the bottom of the screen

6. Now click on the other folder and do the same to the left side of your screen.

Don't you wish you had Windows 7 now?

Now let's move "New folder 2" into "New folder 1."

1. In your Documents folder, grab "New folder 1."

2. Drag it up and over "New folder 2" in the same window till "New folder 2" is highlighted and you see "Move to new folder 1"

3. Drop it.

Notice that you can now see "New folder 2" in your open "New folder 1" window. Now we can move it back. Oops, how can we move it back when we no longer have both folders in the same window?

1. Grab New folder 2

2. Drag it over to the Documents folder.

    a. Make sure you are hovering over a blank space or over the top of the folder so that you can see the words "Move to my documents."

3. Drop it.

Now we will try another way.

1. Right click on "New folder 1" inside your Documents folder.

2. In the pop up menu click on "Cut."

3. Move the pointer inside the "New folder 1" window.

4. Right click.

5. Click on "paste."

We just performed a "cut and paste" procedure.

As you can see, rearranging, renaming, placing files inside folders, making new folders and so on, is not difficult at all. The most difficult part of this process is sticking with your filing plan and making a place for everything and keeping everything in its place. Basically, you're keeping your files clean and arranged.

Deleting Files and Folders

In the last procedure we left a mess. We now have two folders and two files that we do not need cluttering up our filing system. Let's get rid of them.

1. In your open "New folder 1" right click on "New document file 1"

2. In the pop up menu, click on "Delete."

3. You will be asked if you are sure you want to move this file to the recycle bin?

4. Click "Yes."

The file no longer appears in your folder. The good news is that if you make a mistake deleting a file you can still recover it from the recycle bin later. At least up to the point that you empty the recycle bin.

You may ask, couldn't we just delete the folder with the file in it and get rid of both at the same time? The answer is yes. Any time that you delete a folder you are essentially dumping everything in that folder into the recycle bin. Be careful and always look in the folder before you delete it.

There are many methods to deleting so we will cover some of them quickly with our remaining file and folders.

1. Click on "New folder 1" and highlight it.

      a.   Remember that you can use Shift or Ctrl click to select multiple files and folders.

2.   To delete the highlighted files you have several options.

      a.   Hit the "Delete" key on the keyboard.

      b.   Right click and pick "Delete" from the menu.

      c.   Click the "Organize" tab at the top and click "Delete" in the menu.

      d.   Drag the selected folder over the recycle bin and drop it.

      e.   On the keyboard hold the Ctrl key and press the letter D.

I am sure there are more ways, but 5 should be enough.

Recovering Deleted Files and Folders

If you inadvertently delete a file that you did not want to lose, you still have a chance to retrieve it from the recycle bin. The truth is that the recycle bin is simply a folder with some special properties. Mainly, it is the only folder that when emptied or when something is deleted from it, it is gone. Now we will look at how you recover,

1.   Double click (open) the recycle bin.

2.   Find the file you wish to recover and right click on it.

3.   From the menu click on "Restore."

Your file or folder will return to the original location in the same condition it was in when you deleted it. In other words, it you delete a folder that is full of files, it will be restored with the files intact. You also have the option at the top bar of the recycle bin to restore all items or, using your multi select skills you can restore multiple files at the same time.

Security

Any time you allow the general public to access anyplace, you open it up to security risks. Add to this the ability to be totally anonymous and you are asking for trouble. For this reason, many levels of security have to be in place for your protection.

I would not discourage anyone from experiencing the vast knowledge and pure entertainment that can be found on the internet. Treated like real life, I still believe that the internet is a safe place. What I mean by this is, just as you would not leave your front door of your house open when you were not home, nor should you leave your computer files open to others. Just as you would not allow your young daughter to wander in the park alone at night, you should also not allow her to wander around the internet unsupervised. On the other hand, sometimes even with the protections in place things happen. You can lock your door when you leave and someone could still break in. This is why you add the extra security of not keeping large amounts of cash in your house in the open. Likewise, if you are making a purchase or doing online banking, you need to be aware of the web sites security.

Many layers of security are built into your computer and the internet and you do not need to concern yourself with them. Many good honest people are out there policing the bad guys every day and there job is to stay one step ahead. Sometimes the bad guys will one up the good guys and slip one past, but within days the good guys patch the holes and secure you once again. Beyond this, you have the responsibility to follow a few additional steps to be secure.

Antivirus

Step 1: You should install and use an antivirus program. There are many available and price is not the number one determinate of quality. There are many good reviewers out there and you can use the search skills you will learn in the internet section of this book to do your research. Always remember to know who the reviewer is and what they have to gain before trusting what you read. Generally you can trust someone like Consumer Reports or other computer magazines such as Cnet. You should avoid reviews printed or sponsored by a manufacturer. The fact is, if you ask 10 people what is the best antivirus you could get up to 10 different answers. I will go so far as to say that Microsoft Security Essentials has gotten great reviews, it is free, and it is backed by Microsoft knowledge and money. Always update your virus definitions every day. The bad guys update the infections every day so you have to keep up.

Updates

Step 2: Keep ALL of your software up to date with fixes and patches from the manufacturer. Windows has a setting built in that checks for updates automatically and you should always have this turned on. To check this you should follow these steps.

1. Click on the Start or Windows button.

2. Type "Turn automatic updating on or off" in the search box.

3. In the selection box under important updates select "Install updates automatically."

4. Select "Every day" in the next box.

5. Select a time.

    a. Any time will do but it is best to do it before doing your main computer work.

6. Check the Recommended updates box.

7. Select who can install updates.

8. Select the Microsoft Updates box.

9. The last box is up to you.

    a. Sometimes the detailed notification is more than the average user needs to know.

10. Click on OK.

For software other than your operating system you can check with the programs web site or look in the help files to see if they have an auto setting. There are free programs out there that will check for you and keep you up to date on all of your programs automatically. I use and recommend one called Secunia Personal Software Inspector (PSI) which is available from their web site http://secunia.com/products/. They also have an online version (OSI) that you do not have to install, but you have to remember to come back and use it regularly.

Attachments

Step 3: Use care when reading email with attachments. Clicking on attachments to open then could launch a malware and do damage to your computer. In the section on email we will delve deeper into this subject.

Backup

Step 4: Backups or backing up your data is simply making a copy of your data so that if...when something happens to your computer or hard drive, you can minimize your loss. Yes I did say "when" for a reason. Let me share an experience.

Some time back I received a call from a client and was asked to take a look at her laptop. It was making some "funny noises" every once in a while. After hearing the sound I told her it was something I have never heard but concluding that the hard drive is the only moving part inside a laptop besides the fan, and the fan was working fine, the odds were that it was starting to fail. The next question that I asked was when was your last backup? Like normal, the answer was in the form of a question, "backup, what is that?" I immediately started a full backup while explaining what I was doing. Sure enough, less than ¼ of the way into it the hard drive experienced a catastrophic failure. No matter what we tried, the drive would not respond.

The client was not concerned. A new hard drive is not too expensive and there was nothing very important saved on the old drive. Over the next week I received approximately five calls from this client and each time she was remembering things that she had saved on the drive. First was the email address of all of her friends. No problem, that can be rebuilt by making several calls and getting lists from other people. Then came the realization that the only copies of the pictures from day one of the new grand babies life and the graduation of her son were on that drive. Gone forever, and preventable with a little planning and a backup. The moral is, even if you think you have nothing of any importance on your drive the odds are that you do.

Backing up can be as simple as making copies of important files to an external media, CD or DVD or flash drive, or as in depth as making a complete copy of your entire hard drive to a different drive or a tape drive. In most cases, a beginner user will not need to copy all of the programs because you will have the original copy that you loaded from. You may however need to back up your operating system. In the past, new computers came with discs to recover your computer to its "factory state" if you have problems, but if you purchase a new computer today you will need to make a system recovery disc. The steps to do this are automatically displayed on your new computer the first time you turn it on and set it up, but if you are past this and did not do it, here are the steps. Remember, this is for Windows 7 and Vista users.

1. Click on the Start or Windows button.

2. Type "Recovery disc creation."

a. This is sometimes called "Create a system recovery disc."

b. Remember that you can type the first few letters and stop.

3. Click on the program link, it should be at the top of the menu.

4. If you get the user account control warning click on "Allow."

5. Place a blank CDR or DVDR into your drive.

6. Follow the on screen instructions.

Once this disc is created, label it and put it away where you can find it if you ever need to. Hopefully you never will, but having it could save you a lot of time and money.

To back up your files and data you will need to first develop a plan. Based on the importance of your data, how often you change or save new data, and the cost involved in replacing your data, you can create a plan that suits you. Your plan will include when to backup and what to backup. When to backup is the easy question. If you add or change data every day and you can't afford to lose any of it, backup every day. If you seldom make any changes and the information is noncritical, then monthly or even longer may suit you. Keep in mind that even if you think you will not miss the data if you have a loss, the odds are you will.

Prior to Windows Vista and now Windows 7, you were better off using a third party program to do your backups. There are many free programs out there and most will walk you through the steps. Since we are focused on Windows 7 and it has a very good backup program built in, I will take you through the steps here.

1. Click on the START or WINDOWS button.

2. Type "Backup" in the search box.

3. Click on Backup and restore under Programs or on Backup your computer under Control panel.

a. Notice that in this window you can also

        i.   Create a system image

        ii.   Create a system repair disc

4. Follow the on screen steps for setting up your backup schedule

    a.   Choose your destination media.

        i.   Make sure this is not the same as the disc you are backing up.

        ii.   Make sure you have enough space for what you are backing up.

        iii.   It is best to store this media in a different location after the backup.

    b.   Pick a date and time that you will have the computer on but not in heavy use.

    c.   Choose between "Let Windows choose" or "Let me choose" what to backup.

        i.   Windows does a nice job of choosing so if in doubt let Windows choose.

    d.   Review your settings and save.

5. Make sure your media is available when the backup is scheduled.

Media types

When choosing a media type for your backup there are a few things to keep in mind. First would be the amount of space needed for your backup and second, the type of drive you have on your computer. Let's look at the different media types.

CD-ROM (which stands for "Compact Disc read-only memory") is a Compact Disc (CD Media) that contains data accessible by a computer. While the Compact Disc format was originally designed for music storage and playback, the format was later adapted to hold data. A CD is a read only media and not suitable for a backup while CD-R and CD-RW are writeable and rewritable respectively. Most CDs will hold 700MB of data which is relatively small compared to today's standards.

Another variation on the CD is the DVD, and is the most popular optical disc storage media format for movies. Again, the DVD is a read only disc while the DVD-R and the DVD-RW are writeable and suitable for backups. Different types of DVDs have different capacities ranging from around 4.7GB to 8.5GB on the double Layer DVD. The main thing to keep in mind is that you have to get the proper format for your drive and you should be able to determine this by looking on the door of the drive.

A floppy disk (or floppy diskette) is an older data storage medium, which has been around since the 1970s, and is composed of a disk of thin, flexible ("floppy") magnetic storage medium encased in a square or rectangular plastic shell. Most new computers no longer have a floppy drive due to the storage space and relatively unsecure nature of data storage.

Tape Media is used primarily for backup purposes, and generally on network servers, and is not much different from a video cassette. The DAT tape format is the most popular now, but in the past almost every conceivable tape format was introduced. Digital Data Storage (DDS) is a format for storing and backing up computer data on magnetic tape that evolved from Digital Audio Tape (DAT) technology, which was originally created for CD-quality audio recording. Tape backups require you to have a tape drive and these are not popular in homes due to the additional cost.

Flash media, sometimes called flash drives, thumb drives, memory sticks, and many other terms, are becoming more and more popular due to their size and durability. The term flash refers to electronically rewritable memory and, since there are no moving parts, this memory can be made very small and is proving to be reliable for long term storage of data. Capacities of flash drives have a wide range and as of the writing of this book 128GB drives are readily available. Most flash drives will plug into a USB port, but flash memory used in cameras and music players comes in many different formats today.

External hard drive cases allow you to use the same type of drive that is inside your computer and make it removable and portable, thus suitable for backups. Capacities of hard drives are now up to 2TB (1TB =

931.32GB) and growing every year. In many cases, a large external hard drive is capable of storing multiple backups at one time. Solid state hard drives, utilizing the flash memory technology with no moving parts, are making the portability of hard drives safer and more reliable.

Cloud storage is also becoming more and more popular today. This is sending your data over the internet to a remote location for safe keeping. You can rent space (some free space is available) or share with a friend where she sends data to your computer and you send data to her's.

Storage locations

When choosing where to store your backup media you need to consider why you are backing up to begin with. Backups not only protect data from loss due to computer problems, but also from other disasters. If your computer was destroyed by fire, flood, storm or any other method, your data will likely be lost too. If your computer is lost or stolen you will also lose the data. The reason for the backup is to prevent this loss and if you are storing the backup on your desk next to the computer or in the case with your laptop, the odds of losing the backup are increased. Also remember that your backup has all of the personal information that you have on your computer so you do not want it to fall into the wrong hands.

I recommend storing your backup at a different location from your computer. By different location I mean, if possible, at a different address. If you have a trusted friend or relative who also has a backup to store, trade them. Another thing to consider is keeping the backup locked up. Depending on the nature of the data, you may consider a safe or a lockbox. Even a safety deposit box at the bank could be used. The main point is how important your data is.

Passwords

Step 5: Use strong passwords.

Here again we need to think of computing like we would think of real life. When you lock up your house you have a key to unlock it. In computing that key is your password. Just as your key has many peaks and valleys along one and sometimes both edges, your password should also be made up of a combination of somewhat random characters. Would you leave your key lying around so anyone could get it and use it? No, you wouldn't. The key for your car, your house, and even your office are all different so if someone gets hold of one the others are still safe. Hiding your key under the mat gives your very little security.

When you are considering passwords you need to keep several rules in mind.

1. Use strong passwords.
2. Do not write it down.
3. Use unique passwords unrelated to all others.
4. Change your passwords often.

If you are like me, you can barely remember what you were going upstairs for when you reach the top step, let alone remembering several complex passwords. There are ways of doing it that are not as hard as you would think. First let's break down each rule and then we will look at some options for remembering.

What is a strong password?

When considering a strong password, you have to keep a few things in mind.

- Use long passwords (minimum of 8 to 14 characters)

- Use a combination of upper case, lower case, numbers, and special characters.

- Never use real words that are in the dictionary.

- NEVER use personal information like address, birthday, pets names, and so on.

Most computer services that require passwords, online banking, shopping, and even email, have their own set of rules. Some have a minimum number of characters, some have a maximum. Some force you to change your password every so often, and some will block you from using any part of your login name. You need to always keep in mind the reason you are using a password to begin with and make it as strong as you can. A key to your house with no bumps would be easy for a thief to figure out. There are many methods that thieves use and each one is getting more and more advanced all the time. As a user, you do not need to concern yourself with all of this, you only need to know that some of the methods being used can crack a simple password in seconds and if a thief gets one of your passwords he will use it to try and access all of your other protected information.

Long passwords are simply harder to crack. If you have ever seen a movie where someone is cracking a password you notice that the answer is coming up one character at a time. That is not how password crackers work. To crack a password you have to try all combinations for the total number of characters. If you are using only numbers 0 to 9 and your password is one character long, you only have ten tries to find it. If you add just 1 more character you now jump to 100 possibilities. Make it 3 characters and it becomes 1000 tries. This is referred to as exponential growth. As you can see, if you were to use a combination of numbers, upper case letters, lower case letters and all of the special characters, then you make it 14 characters long, you would have an almost infinite number of combinations.

We just pointed out why you should combine all the different characters, but what are "special" characters? Hold your shift key and type the number keys at the top of your letters. Those are special characters. You can also add to that your punctuation. In fact, the only excluded character in most cases is the space key.

You may be thinking to yourself, why not use a word and simply change some of the letters to numbers or special characters such as "P@55w0rD". If you thought of it, be assured that a thief has thought of it too and it is at the top of his list of passwords to try. In computer lingo, what is known as a **Brute Force** attack will try every word in the dictionary, in every language, with all common letter substitutions, spelled forward and backward. A program can do this in a matter of seconds or minutes.

"Phishing" and "social engineering" are also common ways for someone to get your password. Your name and address can be looked up. With a few simple questions most people will tell you their kids' names, or their pets' names. Phone numbers are listed in the phone book and online. Someone striking up a conversation at a restaurant could come up with a thousand password possibilities in just a few minutes. Don't use them. The bottom line is if you can think it, it is not a good password.

So how do you create and remember a password? Some of you will have one or two passwords to remember and others may have hundreds. Let's talk about the prior first. I have seen several suggestions over the years on how to create a strong password that you can remember, but I think the best is this one that I found on a Microsoft web site,

http://www.microsoft.com/protect/fraud/passwords/create.aspx .

What to do	Suggestion	Example
Start with a sentence or two (about 10 words total).	Think of something meaningful to you.	Long and complex passwords are safest. I keep mine secret. (10 words)
Turn your sentences into a row of letters.	Use the first letter of each word.	lacpasikms (10 characters)
Add complexity.	Make only the letters in the first half of the alphabet uppercase.	lACpAslKMs (10 characters)
Add length with numbers.	Put two numbers that are meaningful to you between the two sentences.	lACpAs56lKMs (12 characters)
Add length with punctuation.	Put a punctuation mark at the beginning.	?lACpAs56lKMs (13 characters)
Add length with symbols.	Put a symbol at the end.	?lACpAs56lKMs" (14 characters)

If you make the beginning sentence something to do with the use of the password like, "This is my personal email account. I use it every day," You stand a better chance of remembering. Also consider changing the rules in the suggestion column and make it your own. Just remember random is best but you have to remember it. If you are not sure if your password is strong there is a password checker available from the same web page. Just enter your password and it will tell you if it is a strong one.

Now for those of you, and me, who can't remember your name some days. All of the rules are great and I do recommend them for everyone. We all know that you are most likely not going to follow them if you have more than a few passwords. It is simply too much to remember. So if you can't do the best thing, what can you do? Later we will look at some alternatives.

Do not write them down

OK, we all know that this is a great rule and most of us will not follow it. I say, write down your passwords and put them in a locked safe, safety deposit box, hidden in the recipe box in the kitchen of a close trusted friend, some place. The point is, do not have a list of passwords in your unlocked desk drawer next to the computer or on a sticker under your keyboard. If you lose a password most places have a way for you to reestablish one, but it is always a hassle. Occasionally you will find a place where your password is the ONLY way in and if you lose or forget it you are sunk. Other alternatives to writing them down will be discussed later.

Use unique passwords unrelated to all others

I touched on this earlier, but it is one of the most common mistakes people make. If you have the same key to open every lock, to every location, including your car, office, and home, and a thief gets that key, you will lose everything. We all know better than this, but what do most of us do? It all falls back on remembering. We have trouble remembering one password so how can we remember ten? Keep reading.

Change your passwords often

Why should I change the password, if a thief has it I have already lost? Not true. Internet thieves are smart. If someone was to login to your bank and transfer out $1 every month, some of you may not notice for a while. If the same thief did this to 100,000 people he would be a wealthy thief. Sometimes they will get a password and wait for the right time. For example, if they have your charge card password and they see charges being applied from Cancun, they would know that now is a great time to rob your house. Even your email divulges information that would be beneficial to a thief. There are also things called "Bots" out there that will get your email password and use your account to send spam, junk mail, to thousands of people. If this is happening, you would never know. Changing your passwords often does not mean that you have to change it every day or even every week. It simply means monthly or even annually.

Alternatives

Now for the regular person. Those of us who will not or cannot follow all of the rules. Whether you feel like you can't remember or you can't create a strong password. If more than one is too much for you or if you can't remember to change them often. These are the instructions for you.

Password safes or lockers are available. By doing an internet search you can find many good safes that you can download for free. I use KeePass and I would be lost without it. The one warning I will give to you is that with any of these safes a thief would only have to get ahold of the file and crack one password to access all of your passwords. The good news is you only have one to remember so you can follow ALL of the rules on that one. The other good news, you are not using that one password out on the internet so it is much more secure.

KeePass like most good password safes, will allow you to store passwords that you create and will randomly generate passwords for you. You can also set an expiration date so that you are reminded to change your password at a preset time. No more writing passwords down to remember them. For me the benefits far outweigh the risks. By increasing your security out on the internet where the real risk is, you can afford to take a little more risk at home. Just remember to not copy the password file to a mobile storage device and if you store it on a mobile computer, take extra care. By extra care I mean first, never let it out of your sight. If it is ever lost or stolen, treat it like a lost wallet or purse. Immediately contact all of the places where you are using passwords and change them just like you would do for the cards in the wallet.

Any password is better than no password. Use something you can remember. As far as writing them down, we spoke of this already. If you do write them down, keep them someplace safe and away from the computer. If you use the same password for multiple accounts you know the risk, but like I said, any password is better than no password.

User Accounts

Earlier (in the getting started section) I mentioned that you should set up user accounts on your computer. I will now explain why.

The default account on a new computer is an administrative account. You have to have one administrative account so that you are allowed to make changes to your settings and control other users' access. You may not choose to make any of these changes, but without an administrative account you would be locked out of the options and no one would even be able to do work on the system. The problem is, with the right, comes the responsibility. Loading new programs, changings settings, and much more requires administrative rights.

Let's assume that you are the computer administrator and you are on the internet. All of a sudden a pop up window informs you that your computer is infected with a virus and you need to click here to start a scan. Without thinking, you click. Too late, you just activated a scam malware that is now loading on your computer. This type of scam goes by many names and what it will do is change your rights to Standard user which will not allow you to change anything, which in turn blocks you from removing the malware. Next the scam will show you a list of potential viruses that are on your computer and tell you that if you send them $39.95 they will remove the viruses. The truth is, if you give them your charge card account number, they will remove your money and do nothing to your computer. You are now left with less money and a computer that continues to have popup windows blocking you from normal use. The good news is that this type of scam and many others, some much worse, can be limited by always logging in with a standard user account and only using the administrative account when you need to make administrative changes.

To set up additional accounts (if you did not do so when your computer was new) you can follow these steps.

1. Click on the Start of Windows button.

2. Type in the search box "User Accounts."

3. Click on the User Accounts link under Control Panel.

4. Click on Manage another account.

5. Click on Create a new account.

6. Type in the new account name and click on the Standard user radio button.

7. Click on Create Account.

8. Click on the newly created account.

9. Click on Create a password.

10. Enter the new password.

11. Retype the password in the Confirm new password box.

    a. You can also type in a hint to remind you what your password is.

12. Click on Create password.

As you can see, you have more options to customize your account on this page including Parental Controls.

Now you can log out of the administrative account and log in as a standard user. As a standard user, if you were to click on the same link in the popup you will be asked to type in the administrator's password. You can still download the malware if you type the password, but it gives you that one extra layer of protection and time to think about what you are doing. There are other threats that do not require a click that could load if you are logged in as administrator, so the recommendation is, never use the administrator account without a reason.

Smart surfing

Step 6: Surf smart. I considered putting this section in the chapter called The Internet, but realized that it is too important and needs to be part of security.

Think of the internet like you think of a shopping mall. Generally it is a safe place to be, but you do have to take some precautions. You would not leave your car unlocked in the parking lot, you would not leave your purse or wallet lying out on the counter, and you would not give your personal information and Social Security number to a stranger walking past. The same applies when we are on the internet. You do not need to live in fear, so long as you surf smart.

We all know that if we go to the bad part of town or hang out in a dark parking garage we will increase our risk of getting robbed or attacked. The same is true in the internet. The majority of the bad guys are right where you would expect them to be. In the dark corners of the web. The thing is that the majority are not the ones we need to be most concerned about. The majority of the bad guys out there are an annoyance and the problems that they create are viruses and scams. A good antivirus and a little thought about what you are clicking on will protect you in most cases. The minority, the high end bad guys, are the ones to watch out for. Again, the internet is safe, so long as you take a little care. If you are going to buy online or do any type of banking online, there are a few things to keep in mind.

- Never go to banking sites, shopping sites, or other financial transaction sites from a link in an email. Links can be made to look like you are going one place when in fact they can send you to a clone site owned and operated as a scam. For a sample of this kind of email see Figure 18. The site looks like your bank's site and when you enter your login name and password they can redirect you back to your bank. You think you just made a mistake logging in when in fact you just gave your login information to a bad guy.

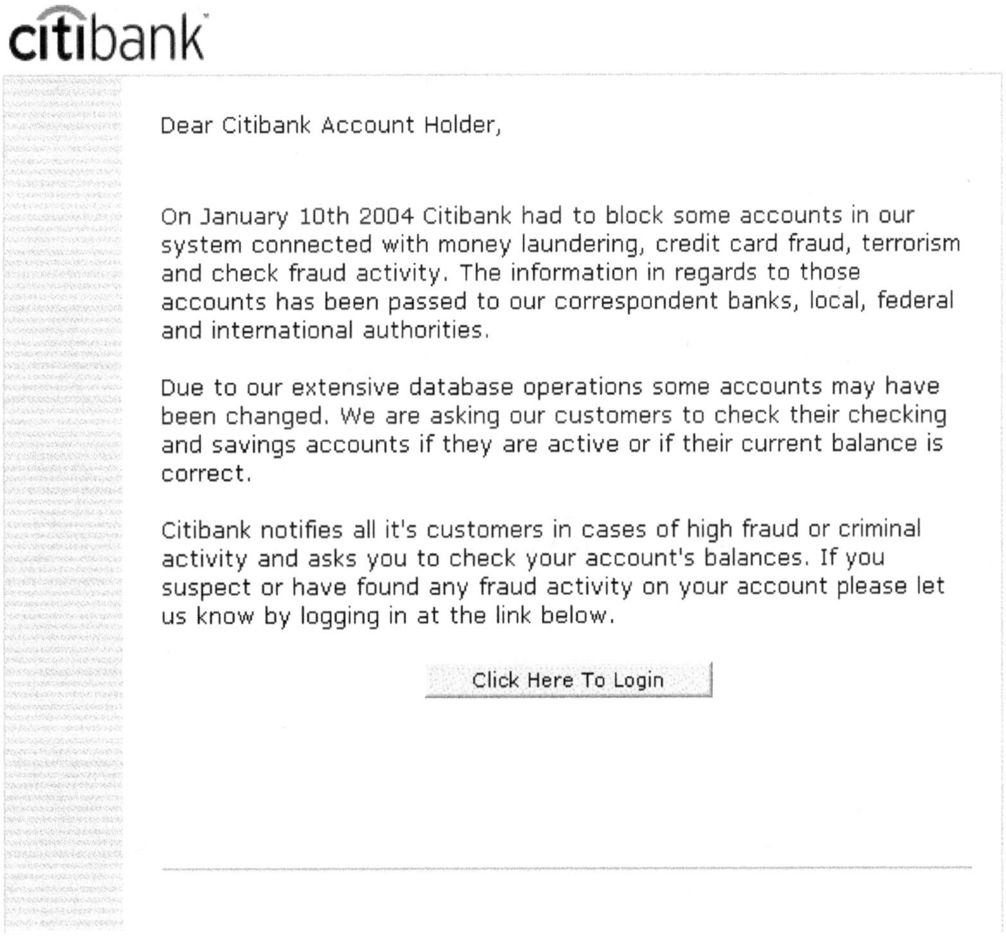

citibank

Dear Citibank Account Holder,

On January 10th 2004 Citibank had to block some accounts in our system connected with money laundering, credit card fraud, terrorism and check fraud activity. The information in regards to those accounts has been passed to our correspondent banks, local, federal and international authorities.

Due to our extensive database operations some accounts may have been changed. We are asking our customers to check their checking and savings accounts if they are active or if their current balance is correct.

Citibank notifies all it's customers in cases of high fraud or criminal activity and asks you to check your account's balances. If you suspect or have found any fraud activity on your account please let us know by logging in at the link below.

| Click Here To Login |

Figure 17

- Always look at the address bar when logging in. If the bank or other sites name is spelled wrong or is not even in the address, you may be at a clone site.

- Look for the gold padlock. In Internet Explorer it is to the right of the address (see Figure 19) and in Firefox it is in the lower right corner. Others may have it elsewhere. If you click on the

Figure 19

padlock you will get a Verisign Certificate (Figure 20) message which tells you who the certificate is issued to, the dates that it is valid, and a lot more. VeriSign is the number one authentication service for the internet and if you see a VeriSign certificate they have checked the site and its owner for authenticity. You may also see a VeriSign Trusted logo on the site that you can click and see information about the site.

- Never use a debit card for online purchases. Credit cards have built in protections and limits to how much loss you can endure before you are no longer liable. The only limit to your debit card is the amount in your account and any overdraft allowance. In other words, if a thief got your card and access number they could bleed you dry.

Be smart and when in doubt, get out. You can always call someone and verify that you are in the right place.

Figure 20

The Internet

The Internet is a world-wide network that connects millions of computers to share and exchange data, news, opinions, and research results.

Many years ago the government was concerned that, in a time of war, someone could cut communication from one point to another simply by severing one line. In response to this, alternative routes were established to protect from this loss. Soon other duplicates were set up and after a while this alternative route system began to look like a spider web. From Washington D.C. to Chicago, we had lines going through New York, Atlanta, Indianapolis, Dallas, San Francisco, and so on. Soon the concern was a mass destruction in the middle of the country so lines of communication were opened up going the other direction and we now have a "world-wide-web" of communication.

Like any new technology, the internet has its good and its bad side. Used wisely it is a source of information like we have never seen before, but care must be taken to use it wisely. Just because something is on the internet does not make it fact. Anyone can post anything on the internet. It is important to know your sources and double and triple check anything that you read.

Every web page you visit has a unique name. Rules have been established for naming and these rules must be followed. These names or addresses are made up a minimum of 2 parts, the server name sometimes called the domain name, and the top level domain name which are separated with a dot. (servername.topleveldomain) Top level domain names are limited and controlled by an international organization called International Corporation for Assigned Names and Numbers (ICANN) and are very limited. Server names are then registered and the entire name is assigned a number called an IP address. There is much more to the naming and addressing process but as long as you understand the basics you will be able to understand how to browse or "surf" the internet.

Browsers

Your link between your computer and the internet is a program called a browser. The one that comes with your computer is Microsoft Internet Explorer (IE). There are others that you can download for free and each has different features, but if I make any specific references in this book it will be to IE. As of the writing of this book Internet Explorer 8 is the current version and 9 is currently in testing. If you are running an older version it is recommended that you update to the current version for security reasons.

The browser is not only the link, but also the controller for your browsing. When you first open your browser you will go directly to your home page. With navigation buttons, address bars and other tools, you can surf the web. Let's learn some of the navigation tools.

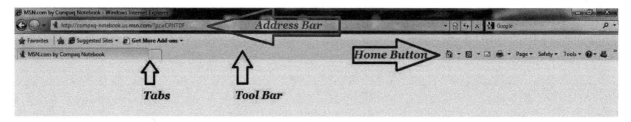

Figure 21

Looking at figure 21 you can see a few parts of the browser labeled with large arrows. The address bar will tell you your current location or address. Every web site has a unique address. If you know where you would like to go you can type the address in the address bar and hit enter. The browser, using the rules of the internet, will go to the address and display it on your screen. If you notice, above the address bar you can see a somewhat more descriptive version of the current address that is being displayed. To the left of the address bar you will see a left and right arrow. The left arrow will take you back to the previous page and the right arrow will move you forward. When you first open IE neither of these arrows is functional so you will see that they are greyed out. Once you start to navigate (and there are pages to go back to) the left arrow will illuminate and if you navigate back with the left arrow the right one will illuminate. Now looking to the right of the address bar you will see a down arrow. If you click this you will see a list of the previous pages that you browsed, a history of what was browsed previous times IE was used, and a list of favorites. Clicking on any of these addresses will take you directly back to the site.

➢   This list can be cleared if you desire.

The next thing you see is a logo that looks like a torn page. This is no longer available in IE9 and was not used often in previous versions. In fact, you can customize your bar so that this button does not show if you desire. If a page does not display correctly you can click this and it may improve. In most cases you should not be concerned with this. Continuing to the right you see two arrows that seem to be making a circle. This is your refresh button. Occasionally you have a page that does not load correctly or completely or sometimes you are on a page that is updating all the time. This sometimes happens when you are bidding on eBay and the time is running out. To refresh the page you can click on the button or hit the F5 key on your keyboard. The next button to the right is a red X and is used to stop a page from loading. You would use this if the page is very large and you wait for a long time and are ready to give up. Sometimes the page will load all that you need and the rest is just a picture or something that you do not need so you can stop the loading and move on.

Jumping to the right of the address bar you will see a search bar. In figure 21 Google is listed as the search provider, but this is customizable and you can have your favorite provider as your default. The down arrow to the far right, when clicked, will display options including an option to find "on this page." That would be used to locate a word or phrase on a web page. To use the search bar you simply type in what you are looking for and hit enter or click the magnifying glass. We will look deeper at search results later. In an earlier chapter we looked at the buttons in the upper right corner but, to review, this is where you can close, shrink or minimize IE to the task bar.

Below your address bar you have tool bars. You may have one or several tool bars on your Internet Explorer and you can turn them on and off as you desire. The more tool bars you have the less room you have for displaying the web page so I recommend being conservative. In fact, the only bar that I ever have displayed is the command bar. To turn on or off tool bars you only need to right click on the tool bar and place a check next to the bars you would like to see. On figure 21 the home button is pointed out. This and all of the buttons to the right make up the command bar. Depending on add-ons that may be loaded on your computer the buttons may vary, but the basics will remain the same. They consist of home, email, print, page options, safety options, tools, and help. Most of these you can explore on your own and discover your options. I will however talk a little about the home page.

➢ Few people know it, but if you ever can't find the control you are looking for, try pressing the Alt key on your keyboard. In IE a new menu will pop up with many controls.

By default, your home page is set by the computer manufacturer or the distributer. Sometimes when you load an email provider's software, or some other software, your home page will change. You actually have full control over what your home page is and you can set it to be one or more of your favorites with only a few clicks. With IE open, browse to the page that you would like to use as your home page and follow the steps below.

1. Click on the down arrow to the right side of the home button.
2. Click on add or change Home Page...
3. Click on the radio button next to "Use this web page as your only home page."
   a. The other option will add the new home page to the existing one as a new tab. We will discuss tabs next.

66

4. Click Yes.

As promised, I will now explain tabs and tab browsing. Simply speaking, tabs are a way for you to have more than one web page open without having more than one browser open. In past versions of IE, if you wanted to navigate to a page and check something without closing the page your only option was to open a new instance of IE. With tabs you can click on the new tab, type in the new address and have several web pages open in the same IE. Each open tab will display the name of the page that it is open to so you only need to click on the tab you wish to see and it will be on top. Closing a single tab is as simple as clicking on the X at the right side of the tab.

> In the new Internet Explorer 9 the tabs will be detachable. This means that you can drag one tab away from the others and it will be in a different instance of IE and you can do side by side viewing. When you are done, drag it back into position and it will snap into place. This feature can also be used to arrange open tabs.

Searching

One of the best things about the internet is the fact that all you need to know is what you want to know. You do not need to know where to look for it; you do not need to know who to ask about it. In the browser section we talked a little about the search bar located to the right of the address bar. Now we will talk about how to use it.

Search engines

Before we get too far into how to search, we should look at what is powering our search. Search engines are the power behind your search. There are entire books on how search engines work and I am sure that they would bore most of you to sleep. We could talk about indexing, Boolean, meta tags, crawlers, and much more. Although that is interesting, once you learn the basics you can find the details by doing a web search yourself. All we are interested in at this time is what to use and how to do basic searching. In 2010 there were three search engines that accounted for approximately 95% of all searches. Google was number one with over 70% (followed by Yahoo and Bing). Why would we need more than one? Search engines search in different ways and for different things. If you don't find that certain "thing" you are looking for with a Google search, you may find it using Yahoo or Bing. If you only want to see results in a certain category, say medical information, you may want to use the WebMD search engine. Although there are hundreds of search engines out there, we will be discussing how to use Google and the information then can be applied to any engine you choose.

You can search by typing your word or words into the search bar, the one to the right of the address bar in IE 8, or directly from the address bar. In IE 9 the two have been combined so soon you will only have the address bar. You may also search from Google's web page at www.google.com. Where you start from is irrelevant, the results will look the same.

Let's get started. As I am writing this, it is early morning. I am ready for a break and I want to get some coffee, but I am in Colonial Motel in Butler, PA. How do I find my coffee? I could type the word coffee into the search box. If I do, within a second I will have a list of about 217,000,000 results or hits. I know this because it tells me directly below the search box. That didn't help, and I need some caffeine quick. By clicking next to the word coffee that is in the search bar I can add to my search and narrow the list. If I add the words Butler PA I notice that right below what I am typing, as I am typing it, I see a suggestion pop up. It is suggesting "Cummings Coffee Butler PA" so I click on the suggestion. I still see about 30,100 results, (Figure 22) but right at the top is cummingscoffee.com. I can click on the link (see Hyperlink or link in the glossary of terms) and I go directly to Cummings Candy & Coffee's web site where I see that they offer a full service coffee bar featuring fair trade organic coffees. Great, but are they open?

Looking at the bottom of the page I see that they have 3 locations and all are open at 6:30 am. Just right, but how do I get there from here. I see that this site has a link below each location that says "Map and directions" and clicking it takes me back to Google but this time it is Google Maps. For training we are going to assume that Cummings did not have a link so we are going to use our back arrow, upper left corner, to go back one page to the original search page. Notice here that you have some options. Near the top of the search results you can see a small map with Cummings location marked. To the right of the map you can see the address, phone number, and some links. One of the links is to "Get directions." That is what we are looking for so let's click on it. Great, we are now on Google maps, which is another search engine that has a narrower list of results. Notice that your curser is in the field at the left next to the letter "A" in a green circle. Google maps needs to know where you are starting from so it can tell you how to get to Cummings. All I know is that I am at Colonial Motel in Butler, PA. I could go find the address on the information on the desk, but I am in a hurry and without my morning coffee I am not in the mood to go looking. Let's type just what we know into the box and see what happens. I type it in, click on the Get Directions button and up pops a map with the route highlighted, written directions to the side, and some alternate routes. It may not be a cup of coffee, but I now know I can have one in about 4 minutes.

Figure 22

We can dig a little deeper into Google maps while we are here. What if I was hooked on Starbuck's and

nothing else will do? In box "B" in the direction search type the word Starbuck's and click on the Get

directions button. You see that the nearest Starbuck's is 14.9 miles away. I need coffee now so I find

the "A" on the map, right click on it and click on center map here. Looking on the map you will see a

slide bar to the left with a + and -. Click on the + and you zoom in on your current location. Keep

zooming and all of a sudden you see some names on the map. You notice that Kings Family Restaurants

and Villa Grande are real close to you but no roads are shown. In the upper right corner of the map you

see some boxes and one of them says Satellite. Click on the box and now you can see a satellite view of

your location and discover that Kings and Villa Grande are both right across the parking lot. Villa Grande

sounds good, but are they open. Back to Google web and search for it. The results show 22,500 hits,

but nothing near the top looks like the web site we are looking for. Next to the map I see a link called

Place page so I click on it. This takes me to another Google page with some reviews and other information. At the top of this page is the name, address and phone number of the restaurant and a link to the web site. Following the link I find that they are not open in the morning so I settle on Kings.

The reason I took you this way is to show you that searches are not without faults. When we first searched for Villa Grande Restaurant in Butler, PA, in January 2011, the restaurant's web site did not show up at the top of the results. In fact, it does not appear until you get to the bottom of the second page about 20th on the list. If I go to Yahoo search and type in the same words the web site is number one on the list. This is because of the way that search engines work. Without going deeply into the inner workings I will just say that the author of a web page has some control over the positioning in the search results. If you go to www.villagrandeonline.com and look at the page you will notice that the name of the restaurant is part of a picture. Although this looks nice, Google's web crawlers that explore the internet and location and index pages for the search engines only see words. Pictures cannot be read by them at this time. This means that if the name is not on the page in words it may not be discovered and thus will not show up at the top of the list. These crawlers are searching 24 hours a day, so if some changes are made to the web site they could position themselves at the top of the results. The point here is that if you do not see what you are looking for you may have to dig a little deeper or even use a different search engine.

What we just learned in the above exercise is that if you are ever in Butler, PA at the Colonial Motel in the morning and you are in need of coffee, look out your window. But what if you need to know how to program your TV remote, or how to recognize frost bite? What if your evil mother-in-law serves you a nice bowl of wild mushrooms and you need to know quickly if they are safe to eat? Searching the internet can get you the results you need quickly, but you have to follow a few rules to get what you are looking for without being overwhelmed.

- Wide searching

- If you start with a single word or phrase, you are likely to get more results than you care to wade through. This is a great way to discover new things, but narrowing your search can save you time.

- Narrowing a search
  - Adding words to your search can lessen the results to a manageable number.

- Boolean rules
  - Many search engines follow Boolean search rules to help you narrow your search.
    - AND or +
    - OR
    - NOT or -
    - Putting a phrase in " "

- Use the links on the search page to narrow your search. Sites like Google have already done some of the work for you so you can look in certain categories.
  - Web
  - Image
  - Video
  - Maps
  - News
  - Shopping

Now try typing in your name into the Google search page. How many results did you get? Next put your name inside quotes. Did that narrow the results? This time click on the images link and then the video link. Are you seeing things that scare you? Remember, this is a whole new world and you have to be careful what you do. I have 150 hits on my name. I check every now and then just to be sure no one is posting things I do not want posted. I have only one time found a not so flattering photo and I asked the posting person to please remove it which was done immediately.

> In the search results page many times the first few results are sponsored links. They are sometimes hard to distinguish but they usually are slightly tinted light orange and say Ad next to them. These links are at the top because someone paid a lot of money to have them there. That is not to say that they are not valid to your search and these could have what you are looking for. Just be aware that they are at the top for a different reason.

E-mail

Email in general is the same as regular mail. You have an address, the sender has an address or return address like on and envelope, and there is a subject and a body just like the letter in the envelope. The routing and delivery of an email is the same as surfing the internet. In fact, as discussed in the beginning of the section called internet, server names and top level domain names are used in the delivery of email. The difference is that all email addresses have an additional name, the user name that makes them unique to an individual person and this is separated from the server name with an @. Here is what an email address looks like username@servername.topleveldomain. In most cases, your internet service provider will provide you with an email address using your chosen user name, if available, and the server and top level domain name assigned to them. For example all AT&T email addresses end in @att.net. You can also obtain a free email address from any number of web mail providers like Microsoft's livemail.com and Google's gmail.com. If you have your own web site or work for a company that does, you may have an email address assigned to you that ends with their top level domain. Whatever your email address is, it is unique to you.

Mail Client

You can receive your mail in a couple of different ways. A computer based mail application like Outlook downloads your email to your computer and stores it locally for you to read. Web based email on the other hand leaves your mail on the server until deleted. Both work similarly so we will base our discussion on the web based Gmail.

Getting an email address

To get your own email address you first have to choose the server name you wish to use. Using the search skills you just learned, check out the features of as many as you want. A simple search for the term "free web based email accounts" currently gets 140,000,000 hits. Remember your rules of how to narrow that down or simply click on one of the first few links. It just so happens that the first link I get today is a list of the top 18 free email services by About.com.   Clicking on this I see that the number one pick is currently Gmail. In the review they also have links to tips, tricks, and tutorials so if you still have questions after reading this you can check it out.

Now that you have chosen Gmail, go to their web site at www.mail.google.com and look for the link to create an account and click on it. A form will be opened that you need to fill out. They ask for your name, desired login name and your password. Notice that after the box for desired login name it has @gmail.com. This will be your email address. You can use anything you want but think about it before you create it. Do you want your name? Not a bad choice in most cases, but if you ever want to remain anonymous it will be hard to do. Also, if you have a common name it may not be available. You can use a dot between first and last name but spaces or other special characters are not allowed. You will also see a link that will check your password strength. After the password you have some boxes to check or uncheck. Stay signed in simply disables the timeout feature. This is not recommended because if you login from a public computer and forget to log out, the next person to use the computer can get your email. Web history gives Google permission to track where you surf so that they can give you more personalized search results. The next box is asking if you would like to set Google as your home page. Continue filling out the form, read the terms and click to create your account. That's it; you can now log on to your web mail account and start sending and receiving email.

Getting to know your email browser

Now that you have an email account you can sign in using your email address and password. Figure 23 shows you what you will see when you first sign in. Notice that along the top left you have links to Calendar, Documents, Reader, Web and more. Google has a wide range of tools and you can use all of them with your one sign in name. After we learn to use the email you should take some time and look at the other features.

Continuing to look at the top bar you can see the name that you are logged in under, a settings option, help and sign out links. The next line tells you that you are currently viewing basic HTML and you can change to standard view. Standard view will give you more options, but for now we will use the basic view to learn. On the left is a list of your folders. Folders are where your mail is stored. Inbox is where all new mail comes in and this is where it will stay until you delete or move it. You also have Starred, which we will not get into at this time, and Sent Mail which will store a copy of all the mail that you send in case you need to go back and look at one. Drafts is a folder that stores any mail that you are currently writing, and any mail that you have not yet sent. In most cases this folder is empty. All mail is just as it says; all of the mail that is in all of the folders is displayed when this folder is clicked.

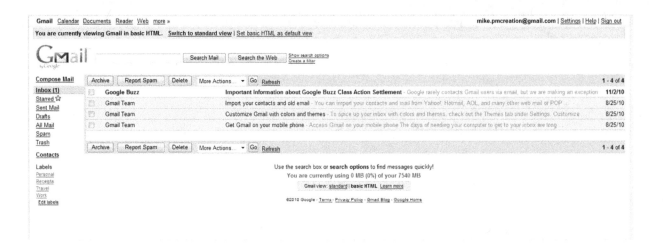

Figure 23

Spam is the word used for junk mail. Advertisements, scams and other unwanted email that are sent to you every day are stored in this folder. Most mail servers have spam filters that quickly review every piece of mail and determine if it has features that look like spam. These filters are not 100% accurate so it is recommended that you look in your spam folder from time to time and delete the mail that is spam and change the setting on the mail that should have not gone into this folder. This can be done by simply selecting the mail by clicking on the box to the left of the email and then clicking on the Not Spam button. If you noticed in the inbox you have a button to report spam. By using these buttons you can improve the filters capability to recognize spam which will help to keep your inbox cleaner.

The trash folder is just what you would think it is, the place where deleted emails go giving you one more chance to save something that you mistakenly deleted. Inside this folder you have buttons to Move to inbox or Delete Forever. You should empty this folder occasionally to save storage space and to make retrieving mail easier.

In the Contact folder you can store all of your contacts and information about them, including their email address.

Reading email

To read mail you can click on the message in the inbox and the mail will open. In the open email window, see figure 24, you can not only read your email but also reply to it or forward it to someone else. These links are at the bottom of the window.

Figure 24

If you need to you can scroll to see your entire email. When you have finished reading an email, you can go back to the inbox on the left side or move to older or newer emails from the upper right link. If you would like to print your email or view it in a window by its self you can do so from the next links. You will also see links to Archive, Report spam, and Delete. In the more actions drop down list you have several more options such as moving your email to a different folder or placing a label on it to make it easier to find later.

Sending email

In figure 24 just below the Gmail logo you can see a link called compose mail. As you might guess, this is where you go to create a new email as seen in figure 25. When you click the link you are taken to a blank email template and your curser is in the "To:" field. Type the email address you wish to send to in this field. If the person you are sending to is in your contact list, you can click on the word "To:" and pick the name from the list. Just below this field you see that you have the opportunity to add Cc (Carbon copy) or Bcc (Blind carbon copy) fields. Simply stated, if you would like to send to more than one person, place all of the addresses in the "To" field. If you would like to send to a main person and also let someone else see what you are sending, for example a team working on the same project, you would have the main address in the To field and others in the Cc field. If you would like to send to a main person and copy someone else, not letting the main person see that others have been copied; you can use the Bcc field.

> ➢ When sending email to a large group of people, some of which do not know each other, you should not place all addresses in the "To" field. If you do so, all addresses are visible to all recipients. This allows each recipient to capture the addresses and add them to his own contact list. This may not sound like a bad thing but consider that is a stranger was a spammer or have a virus in his computer that was creating spam, you are now adding all of your friends to the list to receive more spam. I am sure that they will not appreciate that. For this reason, always use Bcc when sending to a list of people.

After you have addressed your email you should fill in the subject line. This will appear next to your name and address in the recipient's inbox, so make the subject descriptive of the content and short enough to be read at a quick glance. For example, Happy Birthday or December 15th Econ class. Make it short and to the point.

Directly below the subject you will see the attachment line. This will be discussed in more detail later on. Below the attachment link you have your formatting tools. As a rule, in a business email as in a business letter, you should never over decorate.   In other words, save the smiley face four your girlfriend. You should also consider that some people, although fewer all the time, can only receive plain text email. If you send an email with a lot of special characters or special formatting they may see a bunch of unreadable stuff on the page they receive. Simple is best unless the recipient is a close friend.

Now you can type the body of your email. Later on we will talk about email etiquette but for now you can type anything you want to say. Most recipients prefer short and to the point, while others would love to see a long descriptive email. Know your recipients. Once you are finished and you have proof read, simply click on the Send button. You have two to choose from, one at the top and one at the bottom. In most cases your email will be delivered to the recipient's inbox within seconds.

Attachments

When sending email you have the option to attach other documents, files and pictures to the email. This is a very convenient way to share with your friends and associates. It also requires you to follow some basic rules to keep everyone safe. The fact that you can send files means that you can also send a virus quite easily. For this reason you should never open attachments that you are not expecting, even if you know the person sending them. Many times the bad guys will send out emails with hidden virus attachments using your friends email address to send from. Your friend will not even know this is happening and the address capture could have happened when a joke was forwarded with a list of names exposed as mentioned above. Most of these attached viruses are harmless if deleted, but if you click on the attachment the virus is activated. The virus could immediately launch or it could lie dormant for a time, possibly years, and then launch and cause problems. Your best prevention to this is to never click on unknown attachments. Call your friend and ask if they sent it and if it was their file or a forwarded file. Even sending an email back to the friend asking these questions will work. The second best prevention is a good antivirus program scanning your email inbox. These are only about 90% effective so following the first rule is still a good idea. If an email with an attachment looks at all suspicious you can investigate it in the internet. Many times if you search for the contents of the subject line you will find information on a scam. Another good source of information if www.snopes.com. This is a very good site that has dedicated its self to finding the truth in many scams and rumors not only on the internet but also in everyday life.

Now that I have scared you let's talk about how to attach a file. In your email client after you have clicked on the "Compose email" button, you will see something similar to figure 25.

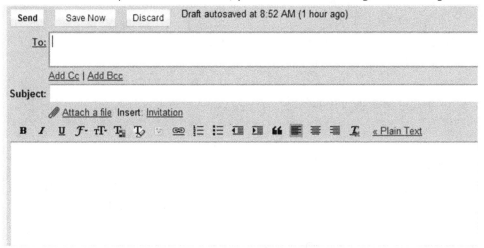

Figure 25

Notice that just below the subject line you see the words "Attach a file" along with a paperclip symbol. The paperclip is the universal symbol of and attachment. When you click on one of these links you are presented with a pop up box where you can choose the file that you wish to attach. You may have to look for it. Navigate to where it is saved and select it and click on the insert button. Remember your skills you learned earlier and if you wish to attach more than one file you can Ctrl click of Shift click to select more.

Now that the file is attached you should move to the subject line and say something about the attachment so that your recipient will expect it. Something as simple as "See attachment," or "Quarterly report attached." Next you should describe your attachment in the body of your email. This will help the recipient in deciding if the attachment is safe to open.

➢ I recommend attaching a file before typing the body of the email. It is very embarrassing to say you have attached something and then forget to do it. Also, double check your attachments before clicking send.

Email Etiquette

As in face to face speech, you have to follow some rules to get your point across without offending the listener. In face to face speech you have the advantage of facial expressions, pitch, and body language that you do not have in email. Here are some do's and do not's for email etiquette.

Do's

1. Be kind.
    a. As in face to face conversation you should consider who you are talking to and speak appropriately.
    b. Remember that foul language or racist comments in writing can be held agents you. Once sent it cannot be taken back.
2. Always include a descriptive subject line.
    a. Keep it short yet tell the recipient what you are sending.
    b. Tell the recipient if your message is,
        i.   Urgent.
        ii. Information that they requested.
        iii. FYI
        iv. Time sensitive.
3. Never overstate the importance.
    a. Remember the boy who cried wolf, if you overstate the importance on a few email the recipient will not pay attention why you do send something important.
4. Keep it short.
    a. Today most people are very busy and get many emails every day.

Do not's

1. Don't ignore spelling and grammar mistakes.
    a. This will make you look less intelligent.
    b. Most email clients have a spell checker built in.
2. Do not over format.
    a. Some formatting, like all caps, portrays emotion the same as yelling. You could be sending the wrong message.
    b. Some recipients can only read plain text. Formatting may be lost.
3. Do not over punctuate.
    a. Five exclamation points will portray strong emotion where one is plenty.
    b. Some email auto readers, programs that read email aloud, will do strange things with too much punctuation
4. Avoid using emotion icons in professional email.
    a. Cute for a close friend but inappropriate for all others

       i.   ;-) = wink

      ii. ☺ = smile

     iii. ☹ = sad

5. Never Spam.
   a. Spamming, sending unsolicited email is not only considered rude but is also controlled by laws.
6. Never forward and email without removing the previous header unless you have permission.
   a. The header will give private information about the prior sender.
   b. Only include the header with permission and to give credit to the original sender.

As long as you follow this guideline you should be able to communicate and not have many misunderstandings. Also remember that anything sent over the internet becomes public. Even if someone deletes a message, copies still exist on the server. Threats, racist comments, admission of indiscretions, have all been prosecuted by using email and social media postings. Think before you hit send.

Appendix A

In Windows you will find that there is more than one way to accomplish most tasks. Using the mouse is many times the most common method, but keyboard shortcuts can also be used. Keyboard shortcuts are a combination of two or more keys pressed in combination to perform a task. Windows has many of these shortcuts built in. Also, most programs have shortcuts that can make it easier to accomplish functions without moving your hand from the keyboard. If a letter is underlined in a menu it usually means that pressing the Alt key in combination with the underlined key will have the same effect as clicking that menu item. The Alt key has many different functions in many different programs and at times, if you do not see a menu you are looking for, simply pressing the Alt key will display more options. In some programs, such as Paint and WordPad, pressing the Alt key shows commands that are labeled with additional keys that you can press to use them.

Below is a list of many common keyboard shortcuts:

Press this key	To do this
F1	Display Help
Ctrl+C (or Ctrl+Insert)	Copy the selected item
Ctrl+X	Cut the selected item
Ctrl+V (or Shift+Insert)	Paste the selected item
Ctrl+Z	Undo an action
Ctrl+Y	Redo an action
Delete (or Ctrl+D)	Delete the selected item and move it to the Recycle Bin
Shift+Delete	Delete the selected item without moving it to the Recycle Bin first
F2	Rename the selected item
Ctrl+Right Arrow	Move the cursor to the beginning of the next word

Press this key	To do this
Ctrl+Left Arrow	Move the cursor to the beginning of the previous word
Ctrl+Down Arrow	Move the cursor to the beginning of the next paragraph
Ctrl+Up Arrow	Move the cursor to the beginning of the previous paragraph
Ctrl+Shift with an arrow key	Select a block of text
Shift with any arrow key	Select more than one item in a window or on the desktop, or select text within a document
Ctrl with any arrow key+Spacebar	Select multiple individual items in a window or on the desktop
Ctrl+A	Select all items in a document or window
F3	Search for a file or folder
Alt+Enter	Display properties for the selected item
Alt+F4	Close the active item, or exit the active program
Alt+Spacebar	Open the shortcut menu for the active window
Ctrl+F4	Close the active document (in programs that allow you to have multiple documents open simultaneously)
Alt+Tab	Switch between open items
Ctrl+Alt+Tab	Use the arrow keys to switch between open items

Press this key	To do this
Ctrl+Mouse scroll wheel	Change the size of icons on the desktop
Windows logo key ⊞+Tab	Cycle through programs on the taskbar by using Aero Flip 3-D
Ctrl+Windows logo key ⊞ +Tab	Use the arrow keys to cycle through programs on the taskbar by using Aero Flip 3-D
Alt+Esc	Cycle through items in the order in which they were opened
F6	Cycle through screen elements in a window or on the desktop
F4	Display the address bar list in Windows Explorer
Shift+F10	Display the shortcut menu for the selected item
Ctrl+Esc	Open the Start menu
Alt+underlined letter	Display the corresponding menu
Alt+underlined letter	Perform the menu command (or other underlined command)
F10	Activate the menu bar in the active program
Right Arrow	Open the next menu to the right, or open a submenu
Left Arrow	Open the next menu to the left, or close a submenu
F5 (or Ctrl+R)	Refresh the active window
Alt+Up Arrow	View the folder one level up in Windows Explorer

Press this key	To do this
Esc	Cancel the current task
Ctrl+Shift+Esc	Open Task Manager
Shift when you insert a CD	Prevent the CD from automatically playing
Left Alt+Shift	Switch the input language when multiple input languages are enabled
Ctrl+Shift	Switch the keyboard layout when multiple keyboard layouts are enabled
Right or Left Ctrl+Shift	Change the reading direction of text in right-to-left reading languages

Glossary of Terms

Antivirus: A software program used to find and block or remove threats to your computer.

Application: *See Program*

BIOS: Basic input/output system. Software that is built into the PC, and is the first code run when powered on. The primary function of the BIOS is to load and start an operating system. When the PC starts up, the first job for the BIOS is to initialize and identify system devices such as the video display card, keyboard and mouse, hard drive, CD/DVD drive and other hardware. The BIOS then locates the Operating System and loads and executes it, giving it control of the PC. This process is known as *booting*, or booting up.

Boot or booting up: Short for bootstrapping (from the old expression "to pull oneself up by one's bootstraps") is a technique by which the BIOS, a simple computer program activates a more complicated system of programs called the OS.

Browser: An application designed to translate a Web page into an appropriate form for human use. Graphical browsers, such as Internet Explorer, Netscape Navigator, Opera, Mozilla Firefox, and Chrome, render the text in a format resembling a printed page, with embedded images placed appropriately within the layout.

Code: A special language that is read by computers to execute programs.

Command: Perform a specific action. Most commands are step-by-step instructions.

Cursor: An icon, sometimes flashing, that indicates your current location on the screen.

CPU: Central Processing Unit. This unit is the brain of the computer processes and executes instructions in a software program. The CPU's primary functions include retrieving instructions from the computer's memory, including random access memory, comprehending and executing instructions, and directing the input and output activity of the computer.

Desktop: The first screen that you see when your Windows operating system is up and running.

Desktop Computer: A non-portable computer that sits on your desk and sometimes has the monitor sitting on top of it. The term desktop is sometimes used to describe a tower computer that sits upright.

File: A Unit of information representing a document, a part of a program, or some other functional object, and recorded on a storage device such as a diskette or hard drive. The term file derives from the Latin word for "thread" and has practically nothing to do with a paper file in a manila folder, yet can be thought of in the same way. Files in storage can be grouped into directories, also known as "folders." Examples of files include a word-processing document, a spreadsheet, a picture, a graphic, musical piece, or even part of an application program.

Folder: Method for organizing files that is related by topic, by purpose, by type, by program, or even by a project that you are working on.   NOTE: When an application program is loaded onto your computer, it will group similar applications in a folder. As you add or create files, you can organize them however you want.

Graphic User Interface (GUI): Pronounced "gooey". Combines text and graphics to make software easier to use. Graphical User Interface features include icons, windows, menus, and buttons.

Hard Copy: Usually refers to a printout on paper.

Hard Drive: Similar to a file cabinet, the purpose of the hard drive is to store information. It allows the computer to permanently retain and store data like the operating system, programs and information data.

Hardware: Is any component of the computer system that you can touch. Examples: monitor, keyboard, mouse, printer, computer case, scanner, speakers and even the components inside of the computer case.

Hit: A search result

Home Page: The page that is displayed when you first open your internet explorer.

Hover: Holding your mouse curser over an item.

Hyperlink: A shortcut to a different place. It allows you to move from one page or document to another. It can be text which is usually underlined or a graphic. When you move your mouse over a hyperlink, the mouse cursor usually becomes a hand which indicates a hyperlink is present. Once you click on the link, you move to another web page or document or to another place on the same page.

Icon: A small picture that represents a programs, documents, and shortcuts. When you click on the icon, the file or program will open.

Input: Any command that you give to the computer through a device. Feedback to a question the computer asks of you.

Internet: A world-wide network that connects millions of computers to share and exchange data, news, opinions, and research results. The Internet is not the same as the World Wide Web (WWW) but is often referred to as one in the same. The World Wide Web is a service that is provided on the Internet.

Keyboard: The keyboard is an input device that allows you to enter letters, numbers and symbols into your computer. The keyboard keys include the alphanumeric keys (letters and numbers), numeric keypad, special function keys, cursor moving keys, and status lights.

Laptop Computer:

Link: See Hyperlink

Load: To install or to activate.

Malware: Malicious software. Including viruses, worms, Trojans, and others.

Menu: List of options that may be commands or other options from which you can choose.

Mouse: Besides a keyboard, a mouse is the most common input device for a computer. The mouse is a small, palm-sized input device that you move across a flat surface to control the movement of the pointer on the screen.

Operating System: Software that acts as an interface between you, the application software (like word processing or accessing the Internet), and the computer components. This includes interpreting and carrying out basic instructions that operate a computer like recognizing information from the keyboard and mouse, sending information to the monitor, printer, or speakers and scanners, storing information to the hard drive and removable drives.

Common operating systems include Windows and MAC OS.

Program: Series or list of instructions that determine a computer's behavior.

RAM: Random Access Memory. This memory is a work area or a temporary storage space where the computer places program information so that it can execute the program instructions and information quickly. When the program or file is closed, the data or programs are removed from RAM

Select: To place the cursor over anything and highlighting it and waiting further instruction.

Software: Instructions that provide the computer with step-by-step actions that needs to be executed to complete a specific task.

Surf: To navigate on the internet.

Virus: A self-replicating software program that is designed to infect a computer by spreading from one file to another. They are spread by attaching themselves to files that are shared.

World Wide Web: Abstract entity consisting of a special use of the Internet to pass documents with automatic references to other documents. The World Wide Web (or WWW or Web) is like a library, where, instead of your reading a footnote and then going to the catalog, looking that book or article up, and finding it, you have the computer do that work for you.

Worm: Worms are like viruses except they are usually spread over the internet without human help.